LEVEL

X

3RD EDITION

VOCABULARY
FROM
LATIN AND GREEK ROOTS
A STUDY OF WORD FAMILIES

By: Elizabeth Osborne

Edited by Paul Moliken
Illustrated by Larry Knox

Prestwick House wishes to extend its gratitude to the many contributors whose assistance, comments, and expertise were essential in completing this book.

Prestwick House

P.O. Box 658 • Clayton, DE 19938
1.800.932.4593 • www.prestwickhouse.com

ISBN: 978-1-58049-206-5

INTRODUCTION

Prestwick House developed *Vocabulary from Latin and Greek Roots* in response to numerous requests for a solid etymology-based vocabulary program. Because the aim of the program is to increase retention of new words as well as to expand students' vocabulary, we chose to organize the Units by meaning rather than alphabetically. A student who associates a root with an idea will be more likely to correctly assess the definition of that root's English derivative.

Each Unit contains at least three Latin and/or Greek roots; one or more English vocabulary words are provided for each root. Unit Nine of this book, for example, includes four roots having to do with rolling, twisting, and turning. When a student reads through the Unit, he or she will see the key letters that signal the presence of the root in an English word. The letters in the first root of Unit Nine form the stems TORT, TORQ. Beneath the key letters is the root word from which the English is derived: TORQUERE, TORTUS. Students will notice that there are sometimes two forms of the root, and sometimes one. The inclusion of two forms indicates a Latin verb from which English has taken two different forms. TORQUERE, for instance, gives us the word *torque*, meaning "a twisting force," while TORTUS, another form of the verb, gives us *extort*, meaning "to wrongly or illegally force someone to comply with a demand." When a root comes from a Latin adjective or noun, only one form will generally be included. Greek roots also appear in only one form.

Beneath the definition of the root, the student will find the word, its pronunciation, part of speech, and English definition. In cases in which an English word has multiple meanings, we have chosen to include only the meaning appropriate to the grade level for which the book is intended. The word *temper* in this book, then, is a verb meaning "to decrease the strength of," rather than the more familiar noun meaning "a person's disposition or mood"; in Level IX, *pedestrian* means "lacking excitement; ordinary and dull," rather than "a traveler on foot." In some instances, students may find it useful to review meanings that do not appear and discuss how they are related to the meaning presented.

If the word has a prefix, or if it is especially difficult to reconcile with its root, the entry will contain an analysis of the parts of the word, followed by a literal definition. *Repulsion* in Level IX, Unit Five, is explained as *re*, meaning "back," + *pulsum*; the literal meaning is "a pushing back."

Finally, each entry provides a sentence using the word and, when appropriate, introduces pertinent synonyms and/or antonyms. For added visual reinforcement of this understanding, mnemonic cartoons appear in each Unit.

Six different kinds of exercise follow the Unit entries. They include three kinds of practice using words in context, one test of a student's ability to infer information based on a word's meaning, one reading comprehension exercise, and one activity in which a student must deduce the meaning of an unfamiliar word based on knowledge of the word's root. By the end of the exercises in each Unit, students will have had thorough practice using the word in context and will be prepared to make the word part of their working vocabulary.

Note: We have changed the form of some vocabulary words to make the sentences and exercises more interesting, eliminate awkward phrasing, and avoid excessive repetition. For example, a noun (*marvel*) may be changed to an adjective (*marvelous*) or a verb (*marveled*).

PREFIXES

A (L.) away from

A (G.) not, no

AB (L.) away from

AD (L.)toward

ALTER (L.) another

AMPHI (G.) around, both

ANA (G.) up

ANTE (L.) before

ANTI (G.) against

CIRCUM (L.) around

CO (L.) with, together *

CON (L.) with, together

CONTRA (L.) against

DE (L.) down, down from

DIA (G.) through

DIS (L.) apart, away from

DYS (G.) bad

E (L.) out of

EC (G.) outside

EM (G.) in, within

EN (G.) in, within

EPI (G.) upon

EX (L.) out of, away from *

HYPER (G.) over

IN (L.) in, into, on, against, not *

INTRO (L.) inside

OB (L.) against

OMNI (L.) every, all

PER (L.) through

PERI (G.) around

POST (L.) after

PRE (L.) before

RE (L.) back, again *

RETRO (L.) backwards

SUB (L.) beneath

SUPER, SUR (L.) above

SYM (G.) with, together

SYN (G.) with, together

TRANS (L.) across

TELE (G.) distant

* Note: *con, ex, in,* and *re* sometimes serve as *intensifiers*. In such cases, these prefixes simply mean "very."

PRONUNCIATION GUIDE

a = track	o = job
ā = mate	ō = wrote
ä = father	ô = port
â = care	ōō = proof
e = pet	u = pun
ē = be	ū = you
	û = purr
i = bit	
ī = bite	ə = about, system, supper, circus

WORD LIST FOR LEVEL X

UNIT 1
conducive
deduce
evince
impetuous
impetus
induce
intractable
invincible
petulant
protracted
provincial
retract

UNIT 2
anatomy
compunction
concise
dichotomy
epitome
excise
fractious
incisive
infraction
infringe
punctilious
pungent
tome

UNIT 3
abject
compel
conjecture
dejected
dismissive
emissary
emote
expel
impulse
motif
motive
remiss

UNIT 4
comportment
confer
defer
deference
deviate
impervious
inference
obviate
proffer
proliferate
purported
viaduct

UNIT 5
apparition
aspect
diaphanous
envisage
epiphany
introspective
perspicacious
phenomenon
retrospective
sycophant
visage

UNIT 6
adherent
diffuse
diligent
dissolute
effusive
incoherent
inherent
insoluble
profuse
recollect
resolute
sacrilege

UNIT 7
constructive
construe
destitute
expound
facile
facsimile
factotum
infrastructure
proficient
proponent
restitution
stature

UNIT 8
complacent
docile
doctrine
gratuitous
indoctrinate
ingrate
ingratiate
intemperate
placebo
placid
temper
temperance

UNIT 9
adverse
convoluted
deflect
evolve
extort
inflection
inflexible
retort
revert
subvert
tortuous
voluble

UNIT 10
approbation
culpable
culprit
decriminalize
exonerate
incriminate
mea culpa
onerous
onus
recrimination
reprobate
reprove

UNIT 11
confide
credence
credible
credulity
diffident
dubious
fallacious
fallacy
fallible
fidelity
incredulous
indubitable
redoubtable

UNIT 12
definitive
infinite
infinitesimal
innovative
novel
novice
penultimate
primacy
primal
primeval
ultimate
ultimatum

UNIT 13
aberrant
circumvent
congress
convene
covenant
cursory
degrade
egress
errant
erroneous
incursion
precursor
recourse

UNIT 14
apolitical
civic
civility
civilize
cosmopolitan
demagogue
demographic
pandemic
politicize
virile
virtue
virtuoso

UNIT 15
advocate
benediction
clamorous
colloquial
declaim
dictate
eloquent
equivocate
evocative
exclamatory
locution
malediction

UNIT 16
acerbic
acrid
acrimonious
crucial
crux
doleful
dolorous
effervescent
exacerbate
excruciating
fervent
fervor
indolent

UNIT 17
annotate
connotation
conscientious
denotation
dispute
disreputable
impute
irrational
prescient
rationale
rationalize
unconscionable

UNIT 18
aesthetic
anesthetic
antipathy
apathetic
empathy
intact
pathos
presentiment
sentient
sentiment
sentinel
tactile
tangible

UNIT 19
abrogate
acquisitive
arrogant
correspond
deprecate
derogatory
despondent
espouse
imprecation
inquisitive
interrogate
precarious
requisition

UNIT 20
admonition
cautionary
cautious
conciliatory
counsel
dissuade
persuasion
precaution
premonition
reconcile

UNIT 21
avarice
avid
bibulous
glut
glutton
gustatory
gusto
imbibe
insipid
palatable
palate
sapient

UNIT 22
fetid
malodorous
odoriferous
olfactory
putrefy
putrid
rancid
rancor
redolent
stagnant
stagnate

UNIT ONE

VINC, VICT
Latin VINCERE, VICTUM, "to conquer"

INVINCIBLE (in vin´ sə bəl) *adj.* unable to be conquered
L. *in*, "not" + *vincere* = *not able to be conquered*
Although the Romans thought of themselves as *invincible*, they were eventually conquered.
syn: invulnerable   *ant: vulnerable*

PROVINCIAL (prə vin´ shəl) *adj.* limited in knowledge of the world;
    narrow-minded
L. *pro*, "forward" + *vincere* = *having to do with a conquered territory*
Rory's somewhat *provincial* outlook made it difficult for her to understand what people in other parts of the world were going through.
                    ant: sophisticated

EVINCE (i vins´) *v.* to establish; to reflect the truth of
L. *e*, "out of" + *vincere* = *to overcome (as with evidence)*
The incident at the mill *evinced* the old saying, "Don't count your chickens before they hatch."

DUC, DUCT
Latin DUCERE, DUCTUM, "to lead"

CONDUCIVE (kən dōō´ siv) *adj.* supportive; encouraging; helping to
    bring about
L. *com*, "with" + *ducere* = *leading along with*
These noisy conditions are not *conducive* to learning or teaching.
syn: helpful, favorable

INDUCE (in dōōs´) *v.* to lead toward some action
L. *in*, "toward" + *ducere* = *to lead into*
Is there any way I can *induce* you to come for coffee with me?
syn: persuade   *ant: discourage*

DEDUCE (di dōōs´) *v.* to draw a conclusion from fact; to infer
L. *de*, "down, away from" + *ducere* = *to lead down from*
The detectives *deduced* from the evidence that the bank had been robbed not long before they arrived.
syn: conclude

▥ *The ancient Romans considered Rome and Italy the center of the civilized world. They thought of people living in the* provinces *(pro, "outward" + vincere = conquered territories outside Italy) as unsophisticated and far from civilization. The word* provincial *still carries the idea of narrow-mindedness and lack of sophistication.*

TRACT
Latin TRAHERE, TRACTUM, "to drag"

PROTRACTED (prō trak´ tid) *adj.* extended in time; prolonged
L. *pro*, "forward" + *tractum = dragged forward*
There was a *protracted* struggle between the two armies.
syn: lingering   *ant: brief*

Though they usually broke early, PRO TRACK stars held a PROTRACTED practice today, running even after the sun went down.

INTRACTABLE (in trak´ tə bəl) *adj.* stubborn; obstinate; hard to move forward
L. *in*, "not" + *tractum = not able to be drawn forward*
Isaiah's *intractable* nature made bedtimes difficult for his mother.
syn: immovable   *ant: malleable*

RETRACT (ri trakt´) *v.* to draw back; to withdraw
L. *re*, "back" + *tractum = to draw back*
When I found out I was wrong, I was forced to *retract* my statement.
syn: repeal

PETO
Latin PETERE, PETITUM, "to seek aggressively; to assail; to rush"

PETULANT (pech´ ə lənt) *adj.* irritable or short-tempered
When I told my little brother to put away his toys, he had a *petulant* fit and threw the toys down the stairs.

IMPETUOUS (im pech´ ōō əs) *adj.* acting passionately and without forethought
L. *in*, "in, toward" + *petere = rushing toward*
Because Barry was a rather *impetuous* boy, he often found himself getting into fights over little things.
syn: rash   *ant: careful*

IMPETUS (im´ pi təs) *n.* that which drives one; momentum
L. *in*, "into" + *petere = rushing into*
The tragic accident at the crossroads was the *impetus* for a meeting on traffic safety.
syn: stimulus, reason

There are many ways to fight wars, and thousands of books have been written on the subject, but one of the most successful types of fighting is called a "protracted war." This tactic has been used by smaller countries against larger ones throughout history. Why might it have been so successful?

How do you think the word petulant evolved from the root petere?

Both impetus and impetuous come from the Latin impetere, meaning "attack."

EXERCISES - UNIT ONE

Exercise I. Complete the sentence in a way that shows you understand the meaning of the italicized vocabulary word.

1.   In order to overcome some *provincial* tendencies in my own thinking, I…

2.   The company attempted to *induce* its employees to take shorter vacations by…

3.   In one of my more *petulant* moods, I told my noisy roommate to…

4.   The army was considered *invincible* because…

5.   A *protracted* struggle between the two countries over land resulted in…

6.   It seemed rather *impetuous* of our club president to simply…

7.   Because we knew that once George made up his mind, he would be completely *intractable*, we…

8.   Many piano players find that loud noises and visual distractions are not *conducive* to…

9.   The governor decided to *retract* his statement because…

10.   Nothing *evinces* the powerful effects of pollution like…

11.   When paleontologists find a dinosaur's bones in an area, they can *deduce* that…

12.   The *impetus* for the riot that took place in the town square was most likely…

Exercise II. Fill in the blank with the best word from the choices below. One word will not be used.

 petulant   evince   invincible   protracted   retract

1.   The _____ debate between the two senators bored some people, but also led to some important reforms.

2.   I hardly expected a grown man to become that _____ when I awakened him at three in the morning.

3.   Harry may be a good chess player, but he's not _____.

4.   When I realized I was wrong, I decided to _____ everything I had said.

Fill in the blank with the best word from the choices below. One word will not be used.

evince   deduce   induce   conducive   impetuous

5.   When Mike saw Hugh and Lena talking and laughing together, he _____ that they were no longer fighting.

6.   Certain kinds of soil are more _____ to growing prize-winning roses than others are.

7.   Wasn't it kind of _____ to volunteer for a job you knew nothing about?

8.   The relationship between the two characters _____ the main themes of the novel.

Fill in the blank with the best word from the choices below. One word will not be used.

impetus   induce   provincial   intractable   conducive

9.   After the accident with the horse, nothing could ever _____ Albert to go back to the farm.

10.   Laughing at someone for having a different accent than yours makes you seem _____.

11.   The _____ for his decision to play the violin was his early love of symphonic music.

12.   Jamie was so _____ that she refused to move her car from the sidewalk even when ordered to do so by the police.

Exercise III. Choose the set of words that best completes the sentence.

1.   The _____ argument that raged in the office for days was not _____ to getting work done.
     A. provincial; petulant
     B. impetuous; provincial
     C. petulant; protracted
     D. protracted; conducive

2.   Can we _____ from the uproar in the newspapers that the senator has refused to _____ his controversial bill?
     A. retract; induce
     B. deduce; retract
     C. evince; deduce
     D. retract; evince

3.   What was the _____ for the supposedly _____ hockey team's decision not to play in the tournament?
     A. conviction; provincial
     B. impetus; invincible
     C. impetus; petulant
     D. conviction; intractable

4. Sam became so _____ that he ran away and climbed a tree, and nothing could _____ him to come down.
    A. protracted; deduce
    B. conducive; evince
    C. petulant; induce
    D. provincial; retract

5. Nothing _____ Ben's tendency to act without thinking more than his _____ decision to become a dare-devil pilot.
    A. evinces; impetuous
    B. retracts; impetuous
    C. induces; intractable
    D. deduces; provincial

Exercise IV. Complete the sentence by inferring information about the italicized word from its context.

1. If one boy *induces* another boy to tip over a garbage can, we can assume the second boy is…

2. If the new family in the city apartment is looked down upon for being *provincial*, they probably came from…

3. When a businessman's boss criticizes him for being *impetuous*, we can assume the businessman has probably NOT…

Exercise V. Fill in each blank with the word from the Unit that best completes the sentence, using the root we supply as a clue. Then, answer the questions that follow the paragraphs.

The American mass media has an abiding interest in the paranormal. Television infomercials advertise "psychics" who convince people that they can communicate with the dead; popular television programs pander to the public's love of occult phenomena; Hollywood produces movies that depict supernatural occurrences as factual. As billions of dollars are wasted on 900 numbers, cable subscriptions, and movie tickets, we Americans must become more critical in our acceptance of subjects and events portrayed as legitimate, from séances and extrasensory perception (ESP) to UFOs and alien abductions.

What could _____ (DUC) so many Americans to part with hundreds of dollars to learn "news" of the future or have a glimpse of a departed loved one? Is it because we do not have the knowledge to protect ourselves from intellectual fraud? Surely, we can exercise enough sense to stop calling hotline psychics after dozens of them have been prosecuted for criminal intent to mislead. Yet, 900 numbers exist, offering mind reading, spirit-channeling, and fortune-telling with monotonous regularity; television viewers continue to be convinced of the validity of telepathy, clairvoyance, and reincarnation.

One organization, the Committee for Skeptical Inquiry (CSI), believes that the mass media plays a predominant role in leading the public to accept paranormal events uncritically. If Americans were to think critically about what they were reading and viewing and were also to reject the scientifically unsupported ideas about the paranormal that the media puts forth, the industry that relies so heavily on our gullibility would be bankrupt.

CSI has attempted to counter these popular media claims. In televised specials, members of the organization carefully explain each step of an unexplainable phenomenon, such as the supposed mind reading of a telephone clairvoyant. However, even when these illusions are revealed, the public has a hard time accepting that mind reading is not real. We can _____ (DUC) from this reluctance that shrewd analysis of seemingly occult phenomena is less appealing than the mystique of the unknown is.

Many people are troubled by individuals who do not take the time to investigate outrageous claims. To the mass media, however, a docile public is a reassuring constant. The general population's inability—and unwillingness—to distinguish a hoax from reality will continue to provide a(n) _____ (PETO) for the media's focus on paranormal activity long into the future.

1. How does the writer feel about the mass media's portrayal of the paranormal?
    A. supportive of the mass media's interest in the paranormal
    B. critical of the media for portraying paranormal activity as unbelievable
    C. angry for creating a nation of non-critical thinkers by challenging Americans to question the paranormal
    D. skeptical about both the paranormal and the media's motives in focusing on the paranormal

2. What can you logically infer is the reason the words *psychics* and *news* are in quotation marks?
    A. The author does not believe in the powers of these people.
    B. The author wants to poke fun at professional mind readers.
    C. The Committee used those specific words in their TV specials.
    D. The author wants to highlight the words for their importance in the passage.

3. Why, according to the author, does the American public fail to distinguish hoaxes from reality?
    A. The media has created a nation of ready consumers.
    B. Americans cannot or will not think critically about the paranormal.
    C. The American public is constantly challenging the claims made in the movies and on television.
    D. Americans are afraid to question the media.

Exercise VI. Drawing on your knowledge of roots and words in context, read the following selection and define the italicized words. If you cannot figure out the meaning of the words on your own, look them up in a dictionary. Note that the prefix *tra* (from *trans*) means "across," and that *e* (from *ex*) means "out from."

The defense attorney attempted to win over the jury in the case by *traducing* the prosecutor's star witness. In response to the claim that his witness was an alcoholic, the prosecutor tried to repair the damage done with a series of questions intended to *educe* a feeling of pity for the witness from the jury. Unfortunately, after the defense's harsh attack, there was little reason for the jury to believe the witness.

UNIT TWO

FRACT, FRING, FRANG
Latin FRANGERE, FRACTUM, "to break"

FRACTIOUS (frak´ shəs) *adj.* tending to argue or cause discord
Malcolm grew from a *fractious* and irritable child into a tolerant and peaceful adult.
syn: cross, peevish   *ant: amiable*

INFRACTION (in frak´ shən) *n.* a minor violation of a rule or law
L. *in*, intensifier + *fractum = to break*
For his *infraction* of the camp code, Kevin had to peel potatoes in the kitchen.
syn: transgression

INFRINGE (in frinj´) *v.* to intrude on an area belonging to another; to trespass
L. *in*, intensifier + *frangere = to break*
Susan said her father was *infringing* upon her freedom when he took her car.

CIS
Latin CAEDERE, CISUM, "to cut; to kill"

EXCISE (ek´ sīz) *v.* to cut out of; to remove
L. *ex*, "out of" + *cisum = to cut out of*
Having *excised* several paragraphs from my essay, I returned to ask my teacher's advice.
syn: expunge

INCISIVE (in sī´ siv) *adj.* sharply cutting; direct and powerful
L. *in*, "into" + *cisum = cutting into*
Natasha's fast-moving narratives and *incisive* style never failed to impress us.
syn: keen   *ant: dull*

CONCISE (kən sīs´) *adj.* brief and straightforward
L. *con*, "with" + *cisum = cutting with or away*
Because I had only one page to write my note on, my language had to be *concise*.
syn: terse   *ant: rambling*

Every law is an evil, for every law is an infraction of liberty: And I repeat that government has but a choice of evils.
—Jeremy Bentham, 18th- 19th-century British judge and philosopher

A surgical incision is a sharp, clean cut; incisive thinking cuts directly to the heart of an issue.

TOM
Greek TEMNEIN, "to cut"

TOME (tōm) *n.* a large and serious book
When I removed the scholarly *tome* from the shelf, I saw that it had not been read for years.

EPITOME (i pit´ ə mē) *n.* the best or most typical example
G. *epi*, "upon" + *temnein = to cut upon*
I hardly think I am the *epitome* of good citizenship because I'm not even a registered voter.
syn: embodiment

DICHOTOMY (dī kot´ ə mē) *n.* two opposite parts of one whole
G. *dicho*, "two" + *temnein = to cut in two*
The film critic discussed the fundamental *dichotomy* in the movie.

ANATOMY (ə nat´ ə mē) *n.* the structure or parts, taken as a whole
G. *ana*, "up" + *temnein = cutting up (any structure)*
Maurice's *anatomy* showed the results of years of suffering.

▣ *An epitome (literally "cut off from") was originally the book in a series that summarized the other books. It now means anything or anyone who perfectly summarizes some quality.*

PUNCT
Latin PUNGERE, PUNCTUM, "to sting; to pierce"

COMPUNCTION (kəm punk´ shən) *n.* a feeling of regret or remorse
L. *com*, intensifier + *punctum = stinging*
Even after a long time in jail, the woman showed no *compunction* for her crime.
syn: penitence

▣ *Whereas a puncture pierces or stings the body, compunction stings the mind.*

PUNCTILIOUS (punk til´ ē əs) *adj.* paying strict
    attention to detail; extremely careful
Max was a *punctilious* dresser; his hat was always perfectly straight, and his shoes were always shiny.
syn: meticulous   ant: careless

The PUNK was PUNCTILIOUS about where to rip his jeans.

▣ *Just as a punctuation mark nails down a sentence, someone who is punctilious has every detail nailed down.*

PUNGENT (pən´ jənt) *adj.* stinging or biting, especially in taste or smell
The *pungent* aroma of garlic greeted us as we entered the restaurant.

EXERCISES - UNIT TWO

Exercise I. Complete the sentence in a way that shows you understand the meaning of the italicized vocabulary word.

1.   If the president is able to summarize the current budget problems in a *concise* way…

2.   Karen's new boss is so *punctilious* that…

3.   Once some of the material has been *excised* from the film…

4.   We could tell by its *anatomy* that the tree frog was well suited to its surroundings because…

5.   The judge told Tim that his *infraction* of the traffic law would result in…

6.   Wei expressed her *compunction* for ruining my camera by…

7.   Richard's essay on modern American foreign policy was so *incisive* that…

8.   The author of the book sets up a *dichotomy* between…

9.   When the ruler started to *infringe* upon the rights of the citizens, people…

10. Isaac was often spoken of as the *epitome* of good manners because…

11. Darren's *fractious* behavior on the football field and in class eventually…

12. The wind blowing toward us from the landfill smelled so *pungent* that…

13. When we saw Helen leaving with the *tome*, we knew she was going to…

Exercise II. Fill in the blank with the best word from the choices below. One word will not be used.

  dichotomy   infraction   incisive   anatomy   tome   punctilious

1.   Discipline at the school is so strict that even minor _____ bring severe punishment.

2.   A(n) _____ certainly exists between the material world and the spiritual world.

3.   Your _____ wit seems to cut through all the unnecessary information and get right to the heart of the matter.

4.   The author's exhaustive writing on French history took up several weighty _____.

5.   By looking at the _____ of a creature, scientists can see how it has adapted.

Fill in the blank with the best word from the choices below. One word will not be used.

compunction   concise   infringe   infraction   fractious

6.   If Danielle feels any _____ at all for lying about her homework, she should go to her teacher and apologize.

7.   Carol's constant arguing and yelling made her seem so _____ that I wondered how anyone could stand to be around her.

8.   The right to free speech is guaranteed to all Americans, and no one should _____ upon it.

9.   A(n) _____ summary of the day's events will be enough for me.

Fill in the blank with the best word from the choices below. One word will not be used.

excise   epitome   punctilious   anatomy   pungent

10.   Cedric's friends were always telling him to loosen up and not be so _____ about details.

11.   Only a special kind of surgery can _____ the tumor from the body.

12.   The _____ scent of frying onions competed with the many other smells that filled the restaurant.

13.   Grace is the _____ of a type of student known as "well-rounded."

Exercise III. Choose the set of words that best completes the sentence.

1.   Even though Alec had committed only a minor _____ of the company rules, he was punished severely because he showed no _____.
      A. infraction; compunction
      B. infraction; dichotomy
      C. epitome; compunction
      D. tome; infraction

2.   Barbara is the _____ of a well-behaved child and would never _____ upon her siblings' rights.
      A. dichotomy; excise
      B. epitome; excise
      C. epitome; infringe
      D. dichotomy; infringe

3.   For her _____ essays and _____ attention to detail, Victoria was named the best student of her English class.
      A. fractious; pungent
      B. punctilious; pungent
      C. fractious; concise
      D. incisive; punctilious

4.   There was a definite _____ in her personality; on the one hand, she had a(n) _____ intelligence, but on the other hand, she seemed to have no understanding of other people.
     A. dichotomy; incisive
     B. infraction; fractious
     C. anatomy; concise
     D. epitome; pungent

5.   The _____ young brothers stopped their fighting and screaming when the _____ aroma of dinner from the kitchen hit their nostrils.
     A. incisive; concise
     B. fractious; pungent
     C. punctilious; fractious
     D. pungent; incisive

Exercise IV. Complete the sentence by inferring information about the italicized word from its context.

1.   If a man accused of a crime hears that his new lawyer has a reputation for *incisive* thinking, he will probably feel happy because...

2.   If the doctor is going to *excise* the tumor, she will probably need instruments that can...

3.   If Dana's father walks in just as Dana is accusing Gloria of *infringing* on her privacy, he might guess that Gloria...

Exercise V. Fill in each blank with the word from the Unit that best completes the sentence, using the root we supply as a clue. Then, answer the questions that follow the paragraphs.

Albert Einstein's life spanned two important centuries: He experienced the birth of the electric light a few years after he was born in 1879 and lived into the Atomic Age, which he helped create. Einstein is frequently cited as the most important scientist since Sir Isaac Newton, who died approximately 150 years before Einstein's birth.

At first, there was little in Einstein's life to distinguish him from many other adolescents. He failed to achieve a high-enough standard to be accepted into a Polytechnic University in Switzerland, even though his knowledge of physics was noted by the school. However, Einstein was unable to secure a teaching position without a degree and accepted a job working in the Swiss patent office, where he worked for the next eight or so years, during which he published four groundbreaking scientific papers—in 1905—detailing his theories on light, gravity, and energy. These papers attempted to show the relationships between light and electrons, gravity and motion, and matter and energy. They eventually led to Einstein's winning the 1921 Nobel Prize for his contributions toward a better understanding of physics and the universe in which we live.

In the meantime, though, after quitting the patent office, he was able to work as a professor at various universities in several European cities. Einstein was more interested in developing his theories than in teaching, and in 1919, a British astronomer, Sir Arthur Eddington, confirmed Einstein's prediction that light waves would bend because of gravity. This discovery was monumental—it changed almost everything science believed about light; the _____ (CIS) headline in one of England's papers read, "Revolution in Science—New Theory of the Universe—Newtonian Ideas Overthrown."

His fame spread, and Einstein travelled the world, meeting religious figures, politicians, movie stars, authors, and ordinary people. With the _____ (FRACT) divisions in Europe and the rise of Adolf Hitler and anti-Semitism, though, Einstein could not return to Germany, and he immigrated to America and began work at Princeton. In 1939, scientists attempted to alert the world that German physicists were working on a nuclear bomb, but few leaders listened, until Einstein took it upon himself to write to Franklin D. Roosevelt and warn him directly; this advice led to the formation of the Manhattan Project, the United States' development of the atomic bomb.

Einstein published over 300 scientific papers, and his major theories have never been disproven; in fact, in 2016, exactly 100 years after proposing it, his belief in gravitational waves was confirmed. His _____ (CIS), most

famous equation, which nearly everyone has heard of, $E = mc^2$, paved the way for nuclear power, as well as nuclear weapons. Einstein was a committed pacifist, though, and condemned the use of atomic warfare. The man known as the "world's greatest scientist" died in 1955.

1.   According to the passage, which statement about Einstein is correct?
      A. Einstein was a great astronomer who had many theories.
      B. Einstein won the Pulitzer Prize in physics in 1921.
      C. Einstein's pacifism made him disapprove of nuclear weapons.
      D. Einstein was the main scientist who worked on the Manhattan Project.

2.   What does the author reveal about Einstein's famous formula?
      A. It led to nuclear bombs.
      B. It is $E = mc^2$.
      C. The equation is famous.
      D. Energy is related to atoms.

3.   Why didn't Einstein get a job teaching in Switzerland?
      A. Hitler's anti-Semitism prevented it.
      B. He was more interested in theories.
      C. He took a job at the patent office.
      D. He lacked a college degree.

4.   What can you logically infer is the reason Newton is mentioned twice in the passage?
      A. Newton was someone Einstein idolized.
      B. Newton was another famous scientist.
      C. Einstein modeled his theories after Newton's.
      D. Newton proved Einstein's theory of gravity.

Exercise VI. Drawing on your knowledge of roots and words in context, read the following selection and define the italicized words. If you cannot figure out the meaning of the words on your own, look them up in a dictionary. Note that the prefix re means "back."

Although the economy was in the beginning of a *recession*, Arthur Witherspoon was not worried about losing his job. He knew that he had worked hard, and his boss would recognize this. He arrived for work at precisely 8:00 a.m. because he believed that being *punctual* was one of his best qualities.

UNIT THREE

PEL, PULS
Latin PELLERE, PULSUM, "to push; to drive"

COMPEL (kəm pel´) *v.* to force or strongly persuade; to coerce
L. *com*, "along with" + *pellere* = *to drive along with*
The pressures of poverty *compel* many people to do things they would not do otherwise.
syn: sway

IMPULSE (im´ puls) *n.* a sudden, involuntary urge to do something
L. *in*, "within" + *pulsum* = *pushed from within*
When Nick saw the rows and rows of candy, he was seized by an *impulse* to spend all of his money.
syn: whim, spur

EXPEL (ek spel´) *v.* to send out or away
L. *ex*, "out of" + *pellere* = *to push out*
The council took a vote on whether to *expel* the treasurer for his accounting mistakes.
syn: eject   *ant: admit*

Modern psychology defines compulsive *behavior as that in which a person feels forced to act out, yet powerless to stop or control. On the other hand, if a person is* impulsive, *he or she acts immediately on urges and desires, without any thought of the consequences.*

JAC, JECT
Latin JACERE, JECTUM, "to throw; to cast"

CONJECTURE (kən jek´ chər) *n.* a guess, often one based on inadequate or faulty evidence
L. *com*, "together" + *jectum* = *thrown together*
Because you do not know where I was on the night in question, your assertions about what I did are pure *conjecture*.
syn: theory   *ant: fact*

DEJECTED (di jek´ tid) *adj.* downcast or sad; depressed
L. *de*, "down" + *jectum* = *cast down*
After Mac lost the race, he sat by himself on the team's bus, *dejected*.
syn: dispirited   *ant: animated*

ABJECT (ab´ jekt) *adj.* lowly; miserable and wretched
L. *ab*, "away" + *jectum* = *thrown away*
Ellen's *abject* begging and promises had no effect on her parents, who grounded her after she broke her curfew.
syn: degraded   *ant: exalted*

Open markets offer the only realistic hope of pulling billions of people in developing countries out of abject *poverty, while sustaining prosperity in the industrialized world. —Kofi Annan, former United Nations Secretary-General*

MIT, MIS
Latin MITTERE, MISSUM, "send"

EMISSARY   (em´ ə ser ē)   *n.*   an agent sent on a
   mission
L. *ex*, "out" + *missum* = *one sent out*
During the peace talks, the young Italian
diplomat was sent as an *emissary* to Beijing.
syn: go-between

We sent out a SCARY-looking EMISSARY to speak with the enemy.

DISMISSIVE   (dis mis´ iv)   *adj.*   showing little regard; scornful
L. *dis*, "apart, away" + *missum* = *sending away*
The professor responded to my confused question with a *dismissive* wave of his
hand.
syn: contemptuous

REMISS   (ri mis´)   *adj.*   failing to fulfill one's duty; negligent
L. *re*, "back" + *missum* = *sent back*
Do you think I was *remiss* in not cleaning up after the party?
syn: delinquent   *ant: prudent*

MOT, MOV
Latin MOVERE, MOTUS, "to move"

MOTIVE   (mō´ tiv)   *n.*   a cause for action
L. *motus* = *moving (reason or idea)*
The detective had the difficult job of establishing a *motive* for the murder of a
popular businessman.
syn: incentive

MOTIF   (mō tēf´)   *n.*   a recurring theme, subject, or idea
French *motif*, "dominant idea," originally from Latin *motus*
The recurring father-son *motif* in this novel makes me wonder about the author's
relationship with his own father.

EMOTE   (ē mōt´)   *v.*   to dramatically express emotions
L. *e*, "out of" + *motus* = *to move out of (oneself)*
My sister tended to *emote* more than the other members of our shy, socially
awkward family.
syn: dramatize

▥ Remit *means "to forgive" or "to release from punishment." The adjective* remiss *means "too forgiving, too relaxed"—i.e., "slack."*

▥ *To me, the themes of my own life are infinitely more difficult to comprehend than are the* motifs *in a piece of music.* —Anonymous

EXERCISES - UNIT THREE

Exercise I. Complete the sentence in a way that shows you understand the meaning of the italicized vocabulary word.

1.   If the principal *expels* the students responsible for the fire, they will...

2.   The sergeant sent Dan as an *emissary* to the rebel troops in order to...

3.   The actor who *emotes* too much will find that the audience...

4.   After she broke up with Ronnie, Francine, in an *abject* state, told her mother that...

5.   When the police officer at the desk answered my questions with just a few short, *dismissive* sentences, I felt...

6.   Since many of our ideas about other galaxies are nothing but *conjecture*, we should...

7.   A repeated anti-war *motif* in a poem might suggest that the poet...

8.   The documentary about hunger that Henry saw on television *compelled* him to...

9.   A doctor would be *remiss* in his ethical responsibilities if he did not...

10. The *motive* for the theft of the football mascot's costume was probably...

11. Whenever she felt the *impulse* to run away from her problems, Mariah...

12. When Stacy was feeling *dejected*, her sister suggested she...

Exercise II. Fill in the blank with the best word from the choices below. One word will not be used.

   dismissive   motive   dejected   remiss   impulse

1.   There was a heated debate over whether the cabinet official had been _____ in his duties when he did not report the accounting error.

2.   I felt so _____ when I did not get admitted to the university that I did not leave my room for days.

3.   Although the champion golfer was _____ of his caddy's suggestions at first, he eventually gave them a try.

4.   Suddenly, Henry was seized by the _____ to leap from the boat.

Fill in the blank with the best word from the choices below. One word will not be used.

motive	emissary	abject	motif	expel

5.   During the negotiations, the vice president of one company was sent as a(n) _____ to the other company.

6.   The _____ for the theft of the statue has not yet been determined.

7.   The baby birds, motherless and unprotected from the rain, looked _____ and pathetic.

8.   If you _____ the student from school for simply stating her beliefs, you will set a bad example.

Fill in the blank with the best word from the choices below. One word will not be used.

compel	emote	conjecture	abject	motif

9.   Some of the children in the play _____ too much, while others read their lines with no emotion at all.

10.   Since the critic has not read the book, anything he says about it must be considered pure _____.

11.   The high winds and cold rain _____ us to postpone the picnic.

12.   In the opera, the central _____ of despair over lost love is introduced when the heroine takes the stage.

Exercise III. Choose the set of words that best completes the sentence.

1.   The scientific community is usually _____ of new theories at first, saying they are mere _____ instead of fact.
     A.   emotive; conjecture
     B.   dismissive; conjecture
     C.   dejected; motive
     D.   dismissive; motive

2.   The sea captain was almost overwhelmed by the _____ to abandon his ship, but he knew he would be _____ in his duties to the passengers if he did not help them.
     A.   conjecture; dismissive
     B.   motif; emotive
     C.   emissary; dejected
     D.   impulse; remiss

3. While no _____ for the theft of the money has been established, we know that the thief was living in
   _____ poverty and could not even afford food for his family.
   A. conjecture; abject
   B. motif; remiss
   C. motive; abject
   D. emissary; emotive

4. The _____ look on the face of our _____ to the opposing army told me he had failed to deliver his
   message.
   A. dismissive; conjecture
   B. emotive; emissary
   C. abject; motif
   D. dejected; emissary

5. I wanted to finish my paper on the recurring _____ I had found in the novel, but other factors _____ me
   to give it up.
   A. conjecture; expelled
   B. emissary; compelled
   C. motif; compelled
   D. emissary; expelled

Exercise IV. Complete the sentence by inferring information about the italicized word from its context.

1. If Roy learns that Sarah is *dejected*, he might call her in order to…

2. If Jeff, walking through the office, overhears Lucia say he has never been *remiss* in anything, he will
   probably feel…

3. If a scientist records some *conjecture* as documented fact, other scientists will probably…

**Exercise V. Fill in each blank with the word from the Unit that best completes the sentence, using the root
we supply as a clue. Then, answer the questions that follow the paragraphs.**

The First Amendment of the Constitution states, in part, that "Congress shall make no law respecting an establishment of religion, or prohibiting the free exercise thereof." The first part of this quotation is known as the Establishment Clause, and the second the Free Exercise Clause. Since 1791, when the Bill of Rights was ratified, generations of lawyers and American citizens have been testing and thinking about the balance between these two clauses.

The debate over prayer in public schools is an excellent place to see how the tension between the two clauses plays out. When asked about the issue, some people's first _____ (PULS) is to point to the separation of Church and State. They use the Establishment Clause to back the argument that no public institution should promote any form of religion. But others are _____ (MIS) of these claims; they say that not allowing prayer in public schools is a violation of the Free Exercise Clause because it infringes upon the rights of some students to worship as they see fit.

In the landmark case *Engel vs. Vitale* (1962), the Supreme Court decided by a vote of 6 to 1 that the practice of a public school in New Hyde Park, New York—encouraging students to recite a daily prayer—was a violation of the Establishment Clause. The students were not required to participate in the prayer if their parents objected, but the principal of the school wanted each class to say the prayer daily in the presence of a teacher. The Court found that the association between a public institution and an organized religious practice violated the Establishment Clause.

The dissenting justice in the case, Potter Stewart, argued that the allowance of a voluntary prayer did not add up to the establishment, by the government, of a religion. He also pointed out that various departments under the federal jurisdiction of the United States had oaths or slogans that contained religious references. Finally, he said that preventing the students at the New Hyde Park school who did want to pray from doing so was a violation of their right to worship as they saw fit; the Court would be _____ (MIS) and in violation of the Constitution if it denied these students their rights.

Since *Engel vs. Vitale*, other Supreme Court cases have examined the place of religion in public institutions. Where can a person's private life, with its guaranteed freedoms of expression, be said to end? And what can or cannot be kept out of the public sphere, in which no one religion is supposed to dominate?

1. The author uses *Engel vs. Vitale* to
   A. prove that prayer should not be allowed in schools.
   B. give one example of a case that considered prayer in schools.
   C. define the Free Exercise Clause.
   D. show the tension between the First Amendment and the Establishment Clause.

2. Based upon the information here, Justice Potter Stewart can be said to have relied upon _____ to support his argument.
   A. the Constitution
   B. *Engel vs. Vitale*
   C. the Free Exercise Clause
   D. the Establishment Clause

3. The main issue of this passage would also be central to a debate over
   A. whether to use religious language in a federal oath.
   B. whether a principal can decide what language is allowed in a public school.
   C. how many people should attend a church.
   D. a newspaper's right to publish stories about religion.

Exercise VI. Drawing on your knowledge of roots and words in context, read the following selection and define the italicized words. If you cannot figure out the meaning of the words on your own, look them up in a dictionary. Note that the prefix *inter* means "among, into," and *re* means "against, away."

Randy, a tenth-grader, was doing his research for an upcoming speech. He came upon a statement by a candidate for president who, in a debate with other hopefuls, *interjected* the comment that the system of free lunches for underprivileged students "is no better than the slave trade." A smile crossed Randy's face at first, but then he realized that this person was seeking the highest office in the country; Randy was *repulsed* by the candidate's stupid, indefensible exaggeration.

UNIT FOUR

VIA
Latin VIA, "road; way"

VIADUCT (vī´ ə dukt) *n.* a bridge that carries a road or railroad over a valley
L. *via* + *ductum*, "leading" = *road leading*
The ancient *viaduct* washed out in the heavy rains.

IMPERVIOUS (im pûr´ vē əs) *adj.* unable to be affected
L. *in*, "not" + *per*, "through" + *via* = *no way through*
Andy seems *impervious* to criticism, but his feelings are very easily hurt.
syn: invulnerable

DEVIATE (dē´ vē āt) *v.* to depart, especially from a path or plan
L. *de*, "off, away from" + *via* = *off the path*
Once Rick decides on a plan for his business projects, he never *deviates* from it.
syn: stray   *ant: continue*

OBVIATE (ob´ vē āt) *v.* to make unnecessary; to avoid
L. *ob*, "in the way of" + *via* = *to get in the way*
If you take safety precautions now, you can *obviate* some future medical expenses.
syn: prevent

FER
Latin FERRE, "to carry; to bring"

DEFER (di fûr´) *v.* 1. to put aside until later
                            2. to yield respectfully
L. *de*, "off, away" + *ferre* = *to put off*
1. If Mahmoud decides to travel to France, he will have to *defer* his examinations until April.
2. The younger doctor will *defer* to his senior partner when the patient asks a question.
syn: postpone   *ant: hasten*

DEFERENCE (def´ ər əns) *n.* the act or practice of yielding to another's authority
As new soldiers, we were warned to show *deference* to our commander in all matters.
syn: submission   *ant: rebellion*

> ▥ The Romans built an elaborate system of aqueducts (literally, "water-leaders") to supply their cities and towns with water. A viaduct, *rather than carrying water, carries a road over a body of water or another road.*
>
> ▥ The original meaning of obviate *was to meet something that was in the way and get rid of it. Now* obviate *often simply means "go around" or "make unnecessary."*

CONFER (kən fûr´) *v.* 1. to discuss something with someone else; to consult
                    2. to bestow
L. *con*, "together" + *ferre* = *to carry together*
1. Lana *conferred* with the other members of her team before answering the
    question.
2. In a ceremony held earlier today, the government of France *conferred* several
    honors on the general.

INFERENCE (in´ fər əns) *n.* a conclusion not directly provided by evidence,
    but able to be drawn from the facts at hand
L. *in*, "in" + *ferre* = *to bring in*
When I saw the horse tracks across the snow, I made the *inference* that someone
had left the gate open, allowing the horses to escape.

PROFFER (pro´ fər) *v.* to present or offer
L. *pro*, "forward" + *ferre* = *to bring forward*
When the reporter asked for more information, the policeman *proffered* a ten-page
document.

                    ant: withhold

PROLIFERATE (prə lif´ ər āt) *v.* to increase greatly in number; to multiply
L. *proles*, "offspring" + *ferre* = *to bring forth offspring*
Without natural predators, a species will *proliferate* until it overwhelms its
environment.
syn: reproduce

PORT
Latin PORTARE, PORTATUM, "to carry, to bring"

COMPORTMENT (kəm pôrt´ mənt) *n.* the manner in which one acts or behaves
L. *com*, "together" + *portare* = *to bring together*
No fault could be found with my *comportment* during the awards ceremony.
syn: demeanor

PURPORTED (pər pôr´ tid) *adj.* claimed as
    true, but probably false
L. *pro*, "forward" + *portare* = *brought forth*
Tim's *purported* illness kept him out of school
on the day of the test.
syn: alleged   *ant: definite*

It was once PURPORTED that PORPOISES could talk.

Ⅲ Ferre *is an irregular Latin verb; one of its forms is actually* latum. *So, any time you see "lat" in a word (*dilate, relate, *etc.), think of* ferre *and its meaning, "to carry."*

Ⅲ Purport *means "to claim," as in the sentence "He* purports *to have spoken with the president." As a noun, it means "significance," as in the sentence "The* purport *of the message was not clear."*

EXERCISES - UNIT FOUR

Exercise I. Complete the sentence in a way that shows you understand the meaning of the italicized vocabulary word.

1. As the plants not native to this forest *proliferate* at a fast rate, the other plants will probably…

2. Although Lewis was a *purported* basketball star, we did some checking and found that…

3. The president will *confer* with the prime minister in order to…

4. When Donna kept looking at her watch and tapping her foot, I made the *inference* that…

5. The judges could tell that the skater was not *impervious* to the audience's booing when the skater…

6. The orchestra showed its *deference* to the master conductor by…

7. The opening ceremonies of the library were *deferred* because…

8. You can *obviate* arguments with your friends and family by…

9. Mark's *comportment* in front of the scholarship committee will determine if…

10. Although Richard and Leah had agreed to save their money, Leah *deviated* from the plan by…

11. The army's plans for building the *viaduct* were interrupted when…

12. When the attorney *proffered* a written statement by the witness, the judge…

Exercise II. Fill in the blank with the best word from the choices below. One word will not be used.

deviate	deference	impervious	inference	obviate

1. Maddie seemed _____ to the insults she received in the press.

2. Frank showed his _____ to his boss by allowing him to speak first.

3. The _____ you have drawn from the suspect's story is supported by new evidence we have just received.

4. If the basketball team members work on their passing, they can _____ some of the problems they have had in the past.

Fill in the blank with the best word from the choices below. One word will not be used.

proliferate   impervious   defer   viaduct   purported

5.   A(n) _____ was constructed to carry the train over the river.

6.   The _____ prize employee was discovered loading his bag with computer equipment from the supply closet.

7.   The doctors decided to _____ the surgery until the patient was strong enough to withstand it.

8.   If the polluting corporations, already great in number, continue to _____ in this area, the ecosystem could be severely damaged.

Fill in the blank with the best word from the choices below. One word will not be used.

proffer   confer   deviate   comportment   obviate

9.   When I _____ with the other members of the group, I found we all had different ideas about what to do.

10.   If the travelers decide to _____ from their original schedule, they may add several days to the trip.

11.   The tax attorney _____ several documented transactions to the officials who were investigating.

12.   Dr. Jones's _____ in the operating room is never less than completely dignified.

Exercise III. Choose the set of words that best completes the sentence.

1.   Bill's employer said that Bill's _____ was not appropriate for the situation and that he did not show _____ to his superiors.
      A. viaduct; inference
      B. comportment; deference
      C. viaduct; deference
      D. inference; comportment

2.   The candidate's advisors tried to _____ with him, but he was completely _____ to their suggestions.
      A. obviate; impervious
      B. proliferate; purported
      C. deviate; purported
      D. confer; impervious

3. The _____ benefits of the diet disappear the minute you _____ from a strict eating plan.
    A. proffered; confer
    B. purported; deviate
    C. deferred; obviate
    D. impervious; defer

4. Sam could not _____ his project any longer, nor could he _____ a confrontation with his teacher.
    A. defer; obviate
    B. deviate; proffer
    C. proliferate; defer
    D. confer; proffer

5. The scientists drew a(n) _____ from their data about how fast the species of waterfowl would _____.
    A. viaduct; proliferate
    B. inference; proliferate
    C. comportment; defer
    D. deference; obviate

Exercise IV. Complete the sentence by inferring information about the italicized word from its context.

1. If a forest ranger finds that a certain species of flower is not *proliferating*, he might expect that…

2. When Arnold declares that he will never *deviate* from his budget, we can infer that…

3. If the September book sale is *deferred*, it will probably take place…

Exercise V. Fill in each blank with the word from the Unit that best completes the sentence, using the root we supply as a clue. Then, answer the questions that follow the paragraphs.

"One engine is good, but two are better." So goes the new mantra of car manufacturers, and it has resulted in the growth in popularity of the hybrid automobile. With new, dual-engine systems that rely on both gas and electricity for power, hybrid cars are beginning to replace the all-gas cars of the past. Among the numerous reasons for the global trend toward a dual-powered car are a shrinking supply of petroleum, a slowly disintegrating atmosphere, and the need of a growing world population for reliable transportation. For Americans and drivers throughout the world looking to _____ (VIA) the effects of pollution, hybrids provide a perfect solution: they are popular, inexpensive, and less harmful to the environment than are cars with internal combustion engines.

These new cars combine the power of gas engines with the energy efficiency of battery engines. In this dual-engine system, electric motors are used to propel the car at low speeds and to assist the gasoline engine at higher speeds. Most hybrids also use electric motors during rests at stoplights or when idling in heavy traffic. This innovation allows car exhaust to be substantially reduced, causing less air pollution and less noise.

The electric motors in hybrid cars run on batteries that are charged every time the car brakes. The batteries are able to store energy from braking or from the gasoline engine, much like the batteries in traditional cars do. Stored energy allows for more miles per gallon of gas, with hybrids able to achieve distances twice as great as gasoline-powered cars. Fuel efficiency is an important reason for the growing popularity of hybrids, as they save drivers money at the gas pump and help to reduce a growing reliance on shrinking oil reserves.

VOCABULARY FROM LATIN AND GREEK ROOTS

The reduced use of gasoline, combined with lower emissions, has given environmentalists much to cheer about. As one driver noted, "I pay less, and my air is cleaner. Who can ask for anything more?" The recent _____ (FER) of hybrid automobiles on the market and on roadways seems to point towards the realization of this goal. People are driving more, spending less, and breathing easier thanks to the hybrid car.

1. The author suggests that
    A. the cost of electricity makes hybrid cars more expensive to run than gasoline-powered automobiles.
    B. drivers of hybrid cars are environmentally better because they drive less.
    C. hybrid cars are good for the environment and the wallet.
    D. hybrid cars are adding to the harmful effects of electrical use.

2. With which of the following statements would the author most likely agree?
    A. Hybrid cars are environmentally sound, but economically flawed.
    B. The reason hybrid cars are so popular is because of their batteries.
    C. Traditional cars are worse for our environment because they travel at faster speeds than hybrid cars do.
    D. Hybrid cars allow motorists to decrease air pollution without sacrificing reliable transportation.

3. Which sentence best conveys the main idea of the passage?
    A. After years of choosing larger, less efficient cars, people now seem determined to stop wasting natural resources.
    B. The fuel efficiency of hybrids is an important reason for their growing popularity, as they save drivers money at the gas pump and help to reduce reliance on oil.
    C. Hybrids are popular, inexpensive, and virtually harmless to the environment.
    D. With new, dual-engine systems that rely on both gas and electricity for power, hybrid cars are beginning to replace traditional all-gas cars.

4. The purpose of the second paragraph is to
    A. argue that gasoline-powered automobiles are faster than hybrid cars.
    B. explain the main features of hybrid cars.
    C. define the main similarities between gasoline and hybrid cars.
    D. encourage drivers to not stop at stoplights and not slow down in heavy traffic.

Exercise VI. Drawing on your knowledge of roots and words in context, read the following selection and define the italicized words. If you cannot figure out the meaning of the words on your own, look them up in a dictionary. Note that the prefix *de* means "away from," *col* (from *con*) means "together," and *latum* (an irregular relative of *ferre*) means "carried."

Many people volunteer for scientific studies such as those that give placebos instead of actual medicine, or those that test for allergic reactions to certain drugs. The problem in recent years, though, has been that many of these studies are difficult for volunteers to continue to participate in, and while the volunteers want to help, they frequently *deselect* themselves. This reduces the amount of evidence scientists can gather in order to *collate* the data and publish meaningful and accurate results.

UNIT FIVE

VID, VIS
Latin VIDERE, VISUM, "to see"

ENVISAGE   (en viz´ ij)   v.   to imagine; to conceive of
L. *in*, "in" + *visum* = *to see into*
No matter how she tried, Larraine could not *envisage* living anywhere but California.
syn: perceive

VISAGE   (viz´ ij)   n.   the face; a facial expression
The twisted *visage* of the monster costume frightened the toddlers in the room.
syn: expression

PARI
Latin PARERE, PARITUM, "to be visible; to appear"

APPARITION   (ap ər ish´ ən)   n.   an unreal figure; a ghost
L. *ad*, "to" + *parere* = *to appear to*
The first time Hamlet sees the *apparition* of his dead father, he can hardly believe his eyes.
syn: specter

SPEC
Latin SPECERE, SPECTUM, "to look"

PERSPICACIOUS   (pûr spi kā´ shəs)   adj.   wise; insightful; acutely intelligent
L. *per*, "through" + *specere* = *seeing through*
Having praised Kate for her *perspicacious* decisions as treasurer, Nigel went on to warn her of the obstacles ahead.
syn: perceptive   *ant: dim-witted; shortsighted*

RETROSPECTIVE   (re trə spek´ tiv)   adj.   looking backward over a period of time
L. *retro*, "backwards" + *spectum* = *looking backward*
The museum will be showcasing a *retrospective* exhibit of the sculptor's works.

ASPECT   (as´ pekt)   n.   a part that can be considered or viewed
L. *ad*, "toward" + *spectum* = *seen toward*
Not every *aspect* of this situation is negative; though we have made mistakes, we can learn from them.
syn: facet

INTROSPECTIVE   (in trə spek´ tiv)   *adj.*   contemplating one's own thoughts and feelings
L. *intro*, "within" + *spectum* = *looking within*
The *introspective* poet enjoyed taking long walks alone.
syn: meditative

PHAN
Greek PHANEIN, "to appear; to show"

PHENOMENON   (fə näm´ ə non)   *n.*   a fact or event that can be observed and/or documented
We observed the same *phenomenon* numerous times among the songbirds.

DIAPHANOUS   (dī af´ ən əs)   *adj.*   lightweight and transparent
G. *dia*, "through" + *phanein* = *to show through*
The *diaphanous* curtains were lightly lifted by any breeze, no matter how slight.
              ant: opaque

EPIPHANY   (i pif´ ə nē)   *n.*   a moment of great insight; a revelation
G. *epi*, "near to" + *phanein* = *appearing near to*
The doctor's *epiphany* eventually led to a breakthrough vaccine.

TIFFANY had an EPIPHANY while studying.

SYCOPHANT   (si´ kə fent)   *n.*   a person who flatters; a "yes-man"
G. *sukos*, "fig" + *phanein* = *fig-displayer*
The new president of the company was surrounded by *sycophants* who never disagreed with him.

III   *A Christian feast held January 6th commemorates the Epiphany. The events celebrated on this day all have to do with the revealing of Christ to the world.*

III   *In ancient Athens, a law against exporting figs was not taken very seriously. Men who actually turned in fig-exporters were considered pawns of the government. From a general meaning of "pawn, subservient person," we get our meaning, "flatterer."*

EXERCISES - UNIT FIVE

Exercise I. Complete the sentence in a way that shows you understand the meaning of the italicized vocabulary word.

1.   When Kaylee had an *epiphany* about a difficult math problem she had been working on, she…

2.   You can tell that Logan is in an *introspective* mood when he…

3.   Bernard's *perspicacious* handling of his client's trial earned him a reputation as…

4.   The appearance of a comet is a *phenomenon* that can be…

5.   In the movie, the shadowy *apparition* of a pirate ship…

6.   One *aspect* of the current educational system that students feel strongly about is…

7.   Debbie accused Ruben of being a *sycophant* because he…

8.   Michelle *devised* a way to solve the math problem by first…

9.   The *diaphanous* scarf falling over my thick, bulky army coat seemed…

10.   The sunken, wasted *visage* of the starved shipwreck victim made us…

11.   The new collection of works by the author is *retrospective*, intended to…

Exercise II. Fill in the blank with the best word from the choices below. One word will not be used.

introspective   sycophant   envisage

1.   The city council does not _____ making any changes to the existing law.

2.   George was _____ by nature and would spend hours alone, lost in thought.

Fill in the blank with the best word from the choices below. One word will not be used.

retrospective   diaphanous   epiphany   visage   phenomenon

3.   The exhibit takes us on a(n) _____ journey through all the films made by the director in the past thirty years.

4.   One _____ that has repeated itself is the revolt of young people against their parents' music.

5.   King William's _____ was peaceful in death, but also bore the lines of many years of worry.

6.   Looking out the _____, frosted window somehow made the blizzard seem less severe.

Fill in the blank with the best word from the choices below. One word will not be used.

apparition   diaphanous   aspect   sycophant   perspicacious   epiphany

7.   Several _____ of the current financial crisis are misunderstood by the majority of the population.

8.   Was this lovely figure before me a dream, a(n) _____, or a human being?

9.   Suddenly, Rachel was struck by a(n) _____ about why we lost the game.

10.   Ashley believes that saving every penny is _____ because it will protect her from hard times in the future.

11.   The only person who didn't act like a(n) _____ to Gloria was the company CEO's husband.

Exercise III. Choose the set of words that best completes the sentence.

1.   The captain's blank _____ gave no indication that he was capable of making _____ decisions.
   A. apparition; retrospective
   B. sycophant; diaphanous
   C. visage; perspicacious
   D. phenomenon; introspective

2.   In his half-awake state, the young boy wondered if the ghostly _____ in the _____ robe was real.
   A. phenomenon; introspective
   B. epiphany; diaphanous
   C. apparition; diaphanous
   D. sycophant; phenomenon

3.   The geologist, working late into the night, suddenly had a(n) _____ about a(n) _____ that he had never before understood.
   A. apparition; epiphany
   B. phenomenon; aspect
   C. epiphany; visage
   D. epiphany; phenomenon

4.   Even an in-depth _____ display of the architect's designs could not examine every _____ of her work.
   A. diaphanous; apparition
   B. retrospective; aspect
   C. introspective; aspect
   D. perspicacious; visage

5.   The _____ surrounding the shy and _____ young athlete claimed to be his closest friends, but in reality, they didn't know his inner thoughts.
      A. epiphanies; retrospective
      B. apparitions; perspicacious
      C. visages; diaphanous
      D. sycophants; introspective

Exercise IV. Complete the sentence by inferring information about the italicized word from its context.

1.   If Horace makes many *perspicacious* decisions as the manager of a business, the business will probably…

2.   If Denise can *envisage* a beautiful location, she might want to…

3.   If Leo says that Beth should look at every *aspect* of a situation, he probably thinks that Beth should not…

Exercise V. Fill in each blank with the word from the Unit that best completes the sentence, using the root we supply as a clue. Then, answer the questions that follow the paragraphs.

Some members of Congress who claim they want a cleaner atmosphere also support relaxing the rules on factory emissions. Rather than reducing threats to the environment on a commercial and industrial level, they devote their attention to initiatives like the ban on public cigarette smoking. Smoking is certainly a health hazard, but it does not impose the same danger on the public as the threat of industrial emissions does. Many factories have been dumping waste in lakes and streams for years, while the government closes its eyes and ears.

One example of this _____ (PHAN) occurred in New York State in the 1970s, at the site now known as Love Canal. A dumping ground for hazardous wastes was covered and used for, among other purposes, an elementary school. The chemicals that leaked out of the site caused numerous health problems among local residents, and the entire town eventually had to be abandoned. Public outrage finally made the government take a good look at Love Canal, and authorities opened an investigation into waste disposal. In response to this and other environmental disasters, the government also established the Clean Air Act, the Clean Water Act, and the Safe Drinking Water Act. However, still trying to protect industrial progress, the government gave large firms years to implement tougher air and water purification standards. Federal and state governments should have enforced much stricter guidelines for reducing risks to the health of the general public.

The government's refusal to acknowledge pollution problems has forced many small towns to take charge of cleaning their own water without federal funding. These towns have been building plants that turn waste products into natural fertilizer, with which they cultivate their crops. Such plants must often be built and maintained with little or no help from the federal government.

This _____ (SPEC) of the problem should be recognized; the government needs to allocate more funds to assist states in dealing with pollution. Moreover, authorities should insist that any factory be shut down if it refuses to control harmful emissions. As it stands, many elected representatives openly voice the need for stricter regulations, but inevitably succumb to corporate influence in exchange for campaign support. Overlooking the needs of the general population in favor of corporate interests is clearly unforgivable.

1. What is the most important idea you can infer from the article?
    A. People are not as important as factories are.
    B. Politicians need to make pollution a priority.
    C. Factories can be good for the environment.
    D. A clean atmosphere is vital to the economy.

2. What would be the best headline for this article?
    A. Water Pollution on the Rise
    B. Politics Makes Strange Bedfellows
    C. People Take Initiative for Pollution
    D. Pollution: The Big Political Problem

3. Small towns have taken the initiative to clean up their water supplies by
    A. building plants to treat the waste products.
    B. installing water faucet filters in every home.
    C. building better sewers.
    D. electing officials who will take an interest in clean water.

Exercise VI. Drawing on your knowledge of roots and words in context, read the following selection and define the italicized words. If you cannot figure out the meaning of the words on your own, look them up in a dictionary. Note that the prefix *en* means "in, within."

In 1969, families across the country gathered around their television sets to watch one of the defining moments in human history, one that had been *envisioned* ever since primitive people first looked up at the moon. Through the blurred lines on their screens, millions witnessed an astonishing *spectacle*: members of the first crew to reach the moon hopped from their craft and began exploring the strange surface. Astronaut Neil Armstrong spoke the now famous line, "That's one small step for man, and one giant leap for mankind."

UNIT SIX

HER, HES
Latin HAERERE, HAESUM, "to attach; to be fixed"

ADHERENT   (ad hēr´ ənt)   *n.*   a follower of a person or idea
L. *ad*, "to" + *haerere* = *to stick to*
Pilar was an *adherent* of the Baptist faith until about five years ago, when she converted to Catholicism.
syn: disciple   *ant: opponent*

INCOHERENT   (in kō hēr´ ənt)   *adj.*   not able to be understood; nonsensical
L. *in*, "not" + *co*, "together" + *haerere* = *not sticking together*
The mayor's *incoherent* speech about financial responsibility confused the audience.
syn: confused   *ant: clear*

INHERENT   (in her´ ənt)   *adj.*   existing as a natural part
L. *in*, "within" + *haerere* = *fixed from within*
In human beings, the desire to build and create is *inherent*.
syn: innate, inborn

FUS
Latin FUNDERE, FUSUM, "to pour out"

DIFFUSE   (di fyōōs´)   *adj.*   1. not concentrated or focused; wordy
                  (di fyōōz´)   *v.*   2. to spread out or distribute
L. *dis*, "apart" + *fusum* = *poured apart*
1. You can tighten up a *diffuse* essay by removing off-topic sentences.
syn: scattered   *ant: concentrated*
2. The chemist noticed that the colored oil had *diffused* through the water in
   the glass.
syn: disperse   *ant: concentrate*

EFFUSIVE   (ef yōō´ siv)   *adj.*   overflowing with words or feelings; gushing
L. *ex*, "out of" + *fusum* = *pouring forth*
The volunteers, young and *effusive*, all seemed to speak at once.
syn: enthusiastic   *ant: restrained*

You will sometimes hear glue called adhesive. *Remember that, like* adhesive, *an* adherent *sticks to a particular philosophy or idea.*

Just because something might be gushing out or overflowing, that does not make it effusive; *this word is almost exclusively used in connection with emotions. Water rushing out of a sewer during a flood would not be considered* effusive, *but people's sympathies for those affected by the flood might very well be.*

PROFUSE (prə fyōōs´) *adj.* plentiful; abundant
L. *pro*, "toward" + *fusum* = *pouring out (in a heap)*
The reviewers' praise for the young actor was *profuse*.
syn: bounteous

The *PROF USED PROFUSE* words to explain the workings of the solar system.

SOLU, SOLV
Latin SOLVERE, SOLUTUM, "to loosen; to solve"

RESOLUTE (rez´ ə lōōt) *adj.* determined; steadfast
L. *re*, "again" + *solutum* = *solving again*
The firefighters faced the disaster with *resolute* courage.
syn: unshakeable

DISSOLUTE (dis´ ə lōōt) *adj.* devoted to sensual pleasure; lacking moral restraint
L. *dis*, "apart" + *solutum* = *loosened (so as to fall apart)*
Neil's mom disapproved of his *dissolute*, party-centered lifestyle.
syn: dissipated, decadent

INSOLUBLE (in sol´ yə bəl) *adj.* 1. impossible to solve or fix
                                      2. unable to be dissolved
L. *in*, "not" + *solutum* + *ible*, "able to be" = *not able to be solved*
1. The company's financial problems were difficult, but not *insoluble*.
syn: puzzling   *ant: uncomplicated*
2. Because the fibers are *insoluble* in water, they take a long time to break down.
syn: tough

LEG
From Latin LEGO, LECTUM, "to select, to choose; to gather"

DILIGENT (dil´ i jənt) *adj.* hardworking and careful
L. *dis*, "apart" + *lego* = *setting apart; carefully selecting*
If you are *diligent* in your studies, you'll learn a lot and get good grades.
syn: assiduous   *ant: lazy*

RECOLLECT (rek ə lekt´) *v.* to remember; to recall
L. *re*, "again" + *con*, "together" + *lectum* = *gathered back together*
The witness could not *recollect* seeing anything unusual on the day of the crime.

SACRILEGE (sac´ rə lij) *n.* an act against a holy person or place
L. *sacer*, "holy" + *lego* = *one who collects holy objects illegally*
Many people considered the theft of the church funds not just a crime, but a *sacrilege*.
syn: profanity   *ant: reverence*

▥ The verb resolve *means both "to work out" and "to strongly decide." The adjective* resolute *means "strongly determined."*

▥ *The following literary characters all have the quality of being* dissolute, *although in different ways: King Claudius, Dorian Gray, Pap, Falstaff, Tom Buchanan, King Midas, Kurtz, Dracula, Voldemort, Professor Moriarty, Lady Macbeth, Hannibal Lecter, Nurse Ratched, Mr. Hyde.*

EXERCISES - UNIT SIX

Exercise I. Complete the sentence in a way that shows you understand the meaning of the italicized vocabulary word.

1. After Charlene finally decided that her difficulty with the car engine was *insoluble*, she…

2. Kim was such a *diligent* music student that she often…

3. After receiving *profuse* thanks from the people he had rescued, the firefighter…

4. Because he is an *adherent* of a strongly anti-war religious organization, Wilson…

5. In response to the *sacrilege* committed by burglars in the temple, the rabbi…

6. Grace's *inherent* kindness and generosity sometimes led her to…

7. The *resolute* anger of the striking workers toward their unfair employers…

8. The actor's *effusive* acceptance speech revealed him to be a person who…

9. Percy could not *recollect* everything he had eaten for dinner because…

10. Some say the millionaire's *dissolute* habits will eventually result in…

11. Most professional speechwriters try not to use *diffuse* wording because…

12. When the other board members heard the sleepy intern's *incoherent* speech, they…

Exercise II. Fill in the blank with the best word from the choices below. One word will not be used.

resolute   inherent   diligent   incoherent   recollect

1. The witness could not _____ exactly where he was on the night of the murder.

2. Although he was many times smaller than his opponent, the little dog faced the bear with _____ toughness.

3. Amy's dance teacher recommended her as the one person in class who was _____ enough to practice several hours each day.

4. Andrew often wondered if the desire to fight was _____ in his character because he always seemed to be arguing with someone.

Fill in the blank with the best word from the choices below. One word will not be used.

diffuse	insoluble	incoherent	inherent	sacrilege

5.   The colors in the Van Gogh painting seemed to _____ into each other.

6.   Do you think selling goods and services in a holy place is a(n) _____?

7.   The medicine made Sean talk so fast he was _____; none of his friends could understand what he was saying.

8.   The birds regularly eat seemingly _____ material like tough bark and stones.

Fill in the blank with the best word from the choices below. One word will not be used.

profuse	insoluble	adherent	effusive	dissolute

9.   DJ was never a(n) _____ of the "every man for himself" philosophy; he always tried to help others.

10.   While one of the twins was quiet and thoughtful, the other was _____ and energetic.

11.   Before anyone could say that I was leading a reckless, _____ existence, I had an experience that forced me to sober up.

12.   Ben expressed _____ regret for hitting the fence with his car, but he still had to pay for it.

Exercise III. Choose the set of words that best completes the sentence.

1.   Though the math problem at first seemed _____ to Candace, she was _____ in working at it and eventually figured it out.
      A. inherent; incoherent
      B. dissolute; diligent
      C. profuse; effusive
      D. insoluble; diligent

2.   The first essay I ever wrote in high school was so _____ as to be _____ in places.
      A. diffuse; incoherent
      B. diligent; diffuse
      C. profuse; resolute
      D. inherent; diligent

3.   Cheerfulness and enthusiasm seemed to be _____ in Beverly's nature; she was _____ even when other people were more reserved.
      A. diligent; effusive
      B. dissolute; inherent
      C. inherent; effusive
      D. effusive; profuse

4.   The detective said that the crime in the church, which many considered a(n) _____, presented a difficult, but not _____, case.
     A. adherent; insoluble
     B. adherent; diffuse
     C. sacrilege; effusive
     D. sacrilege; insoluble

5.   When my teacher writes the letter of recommendation for me, I hope he will _____ how _____ I was in overcoming my learning difficulties.
     A. diffuse; inherent
     B. recollect; resolute
     C. recollect; profuse
     D. diffuse; effusive

Exercise IV. Complete the sentence by inferring information about the italicized word from its context.

1.   If Liza's mother scolds her for her *dissolute* behavior, we can assume…

2.   Katie's thank-you letters were unusually *profuse* after her birthday this year; we can, therefore, guess that…

3.   If Rachel says Marcus was practically *incoherent* after two weeks of exams, we can infer that Marcus…

Exercise V. Fill in each blank with the word from the Unit that best completes the sentence, using the root we supply as a clue. Then, answer the questions that follow the paragraphs.

During the 1960s, support for the death penalty reached an all-time low in America. According to surveys, only 42% of Americans surveyed in 1966 were supporters of the sentence. Some opponents found it unconstitutional because of its _____ (HER) cruelty. They believed it was a form of cruel and unusual punishment, a violation of Eighth Amendment rights. Although the Supreme Court never deemed capital punishment itself unconstitutional, widespread criticism led to the reevaluation of death penalty statutes across the country. By 1972, the Court had voided forty death penalty statutes nationwide, effectively suspending capital punishment until the states revised their guidelines.

Public support for the death penalty has increased since the 1960s, but it remains a hotly contested issue. New arguments against capital punishment focus on the apparently arbitrary imposition of the sentence and the risk of executing the innocent. Critics contend that the worst offenders do not consistently receive the death penalty. Rather, the critics say, the race of the defendant or victim, the quality of the defense attorneys, and the county in which the crime was committed play primary roles in determining the application of this most severe sentence.

Between 1976 and 2016, 34.5% of all people executed in the United States were African Americans, yet they make up only 13.2% of the overall population. Additionally, 76% of executed murderers had been convicted of killing Caucasians, but only 15% were executed for killing African Americans. Critics charge that this statistic reflects the criminal justice system's tendency to value a Caucasian life more than an African American life. Furthermore, most persons facing the death penalty must rely on public defenders for representation. The quality of such defenders has a direct impact on whether or not a person will receive the death penalty, so someone who can afford to hire a superior attorney has a better chance of avoiding a maximum sentence. Finally, it is common for a person to receive the death penalty in one state, while a person who commits a similar crime in another state is given a life sentence. All of these factors indicate the inconsistent application of the capital punishment in America.

Many people have become _____ (SOLU) opponents of the death penalty because they believe it poses the risk of executing an innocent person. Since 1970, over 150 people then on death row have been released due to the emergence of new evidence in their cases. This fact highlights the alarming possibility that some people not guilty of any crime may have been executed simply because they could not produce such new evidence.

Polls taken in 2013 report a 61% approval rate for the death penalty in America. Yet, as more people become aware of the irregularity with which the sentence is handed out, not to mention the possibility of executing innocent people, those numbers are likely to change.

1.   What can you infer from the passage is the content of the Eighth Amendment?
      A. It protects the unjustly accused from prosecution.
      B. It protects people from unnecessarily cruel punishment.
      C. It protects people from racial discrimination in the law.
      D. It forbids capital punishment.

2.   What would be the best title for this passage?
      A. Arguments Against the Death Penalty in America
      B. Supreme Court Decisions on Capital Punishment
      C. The Percentage of Americans who Support the Death Penalty
      D. How to Improve the Imposition of Capital Punishment

3.   What does the author mean by the phrase "arbitrary imposition of the sentence"?
      A. The death penalty is used too frequently.
      B. The death sentence is used consistently.
      C. The death sentence is too severe a sentence.
      D. The death penalty is used irregularly.

Exercise VI. Drawing on your knowledge of roots and words in context, read the following selection and define the italicized words. If you cannot figure out the meaning of the words on your own, look them up in a dictionary. Note that the prefix *inter* means "between, among," and the prefix *re* means "again."

Out of the several dozen members who are eligible to run for office, only three have decided to do so. Julie, the first to be nominated, is a bubbly and emotional cheerleader. Hank, the second candidate, is a late *interloper* who views this election as practice for next year's presidential run for the local chapter of Brains and Looks. The last candidate, Roslyn, seems to take her campaign more seriously than others do; she has *resolved* to take the office her sister lost last year.

UNIT SEVEN

FAC, FACT, FIC
Latin FACERE, FACTUM, "to make; to do"

▣ *Both* profit *and* proficient *come from* pro, *"forward," +* facere.

PROFICIENT   (prə fish´ ənt)   *adj.*   skilled at; highly knowledgeable of
L. *pro*, "forward" + *facere* = *forward doing* (*going forth; achieving*)
Teresa is a *proficient* harpist, and she's also a wonderful piano player.
syn: able   *ant: unskilled*

FACTOTUM   (fak tōt´ əm)   *n.*   an assistant who does a variety of jobs
L. *facere* + *totum*, "all, everything" = *one who does everything*
In my role as office *factotum*, I served coffee, made copies, called clients, and
managed the company's finances.

FACSIMILE   (fak sim´ ə lē)   *n.*   a copy or imitation
L. *facere* + *similis*, "alike" = *made alike*
The art dealer produced a *facsimile* of the painting that could hardly be
distinguished from the original.
syn: reproduction   *ant: original*

▣ *The word* facile *has a negative connotation, but the word* facilitate *does not. Facilitate just means "to make simpler, to help along." Someone who* facilitates *a discussion, for instance, helps the discussion move forward.*

FACILE   (fas´ əl)   *adj.*   too simplistic or easy
L. *facilis*, "easy," originally from *facere*
The book's *facile* explanation of complex scientific principles will leave readers
feeling unsatisfied.
syn: shallow   *ant: complicated*

PON, POUND
Latin PONERE, POSITUM, "to put; to place; to arrange"

▣ *The* exposition *is the section of a play that explains background information, or the part of a musical piece that introduces a main theme.*

EXPOUND   (ik spound´)   *v.*   to explain or discuss
     in detail
L. *ex*, "out of" + *positum* = *to arrange out of*
We listened to the police chief *expound*
upon the new traffic regulations.
syn: clarify

The dieter EXPOUNDED upon his EX-POUNDS.

PROPONENT   (prə pō´ nənt)   *n.*   one who argues in favor of; a supporter
L. *pro*, "supporting" + *ponere* = *to put forward with support*
Is the governor a *proponent* of stricter gun control?
syn: advocate   *ant: critic*

STRUCT, STRUE
Latin STRUERE, STRUCTUM, "to build"

INFRASTRUCTURE (in´ frə struk chər)   *n*.   the basic framework of a building or a system
L. *infra*, "between" + *structum* = *built between*
The council discussed improvements to the *infrastructure* of the county tax program.

CONSTRUE (kən strōō´)   *v*.   to interpret or analyze something in a particular way
L. *con*, "together" + *struere* = *to build together (evidence)*
Alton *construed* Cindy's thoughtful silence as a rejection of his proposal.
syn: understand

CONSTRUCTIVE (kən struk´ tiv)   *adj*.   having a positive effect; helpful
L. *con*, "together" + *structum* = *to build together (to build up)*
Matt tried to provide *constructive*, but honest, advice to his coworkers.
syn: useful   *ant: harmful*

STIT, STAT
Latin STARE, STATUS, "to stand"

DESTITUTE (des´ ti tōōt)   *adj*.   having no money; poor
L. *de*, "down from" + *status* = *down from a standing position*
When my friends found themselves *destitute* and facing a harsh winter, they turned to me for help.
syn: penniless   *ant: prosperous*

RESTITUTION (res tə tōō´ shən)   *n*.   payment for an injury; compensation
L. *re*, "again" + *status* = *standing again*
After Greg was hospitalized for food poisoning, he sued the restaurant for *restitution* of his lost wages.
syn: amends

STATURE (stat´ chər)   *n*.   level of achievement or authority; standing
L. *status* = *standing*
If you want to improve your *stature* in the company, try working longer hours.
syn: rank

The next war involving technologically superior countries is likely to be fought in cyberspace, with attacks aimed at disrupting electrical grids, banking, businesses, travel, security, telecommunications, and other non-traditional forms of infrastructure.

We must accept life for what it actually is—a challenge without which we should never know of what stuff we are made, or grow to our full stature. —Robert Louis Stevenson

EXERCISES – UNIT SEVEN

Exercise I. Complete the sentence in a way that shows you understand the meaning of the italicized vocabulary word.

1.   Julie's *stature* in the drama club was improved by…

2.   When I finally became *proficient* in Spanish, I was able to…

3.   Having listened to her dance teacher's *constructive* comments on posture, Nina…

4.   Jeanine was often called the family's *factotum* because she…

5.   The *infrastructure* of our national banking system could be severely damaged by…

6.   After they were forced out of their apartment, the *destitute* family members…

7.   Marvin's tiny *facsimile* of the pirate ship was imperfect because…

8.   As she *expounded* upon the root causes of the Civil War, the historian…

9.   As *restitution* for the mental trauma he had endured at his workplace, Harlan received…

10.   Thomas *construed* almost every situation as negative because…

11.   As a *proponent* of major improvements to our public schools, Governor Morris believes that…

12.   The audience reacted to the speaker's *facile* explanation of the economic problem by…

Exercise II. Fill in the blank with the best word from the choices below. One word will not be used.

proficient   restitution   construe   constructive   infrastructure

1.   The basic _____ of the community may be undermined by the prolonged garbage collectors' strike.

2.   When Avram learned he was responsible for the damage to the store, he offered his services there as _____.

3.   Until you become a(n) _____ marksman, you shouldn't go shooting outside the range.

4.   Many experts _____ the prime minister's remarks as meaning he will make changes in his economic policy.

Fill in the blank with the best word from the choices below. One word will not be used.

      facile   stature   expound   proficient

5.   Tim's essay impressed his teacher because it was complex rather than _____.

6.   Though Maggie has not been in our club for a year, in our opinion, her high _____ has not changed.

7.   If he had an audience, Alton could _____ for hours upon the glories of ancient Rome.

Fill in the blank with the best word from the choices below. One word will not be used.

      constructive   facsimile   construe   destitute   factotum   proponent

8.   The manufacturer specializes in cheap _____ of designer clothing.

9.   The new hockey coach insists that our comments to each other be _____ and positive, rather than vicious and negative.

10.   The tornado left many members of the impoverished community completely _____.

11.   Although I am no _____ of raising taxes, I don't see any other way of obtaining money for our schools.

12.   Kendra bellowed, "I am not your personal _____; I am your partner, so stop treating me disrespectfully!"

Exercise III. Choose the set of words that best completes the sentence.

1.   Bill is such a positive guy that even when he found himself completely _____, he did not _____ the situation as anything difficult.
    A. proficient; expound
    B. destitute; construe
    C. proficient; construe
    D. facile; expound

2.   The speaker, a _____ of expanding the national park system, began to _____ upon the need for wildlife preservation.
    A. proponent; expound
    B. stature; construe
    C. proponent; construe
    D. facsimile; expound

3. The lawsuits have gone back and forth so many times between the two parties that we must now ask whether it is _____ for either of them to demand _____.
    A. destitute; stature
    B. constructive; restitution
    C. proficient; restitution
    D. constructive; stature

4. The art critic's _____ among her peers increased when she revealed that the painting was a(n) _____ instead of an original.
    A. proponent; infrastructure
    B. stature; restitution
    C. infrastructure; facsimile
    D. stature; facsimile

5. If the manager is _____ enough in Japanese, he can discuss the _____ of the trading plan with the businessman from Tokyo.
    A. destitute; stature
    B. proficient; infrastructure
    C. constructive; stature
    D. constructive; restitution

Exercise IV. Complete the sentence by inferring information about the italicized word from its context.

1. Luke is the *factotum* at the local zoo; his job probably includes…

2. When the senator declares that he will never be a *proponent* of a law that bans smoking, journalists will probably infer that he favors…

3. When a company decides upon *restitution* in the case of an employee injured on the job, the company probably feels that…

Exercise V. Fill in each blank with the word from the Unit that best completes the sentence, using the root we supply as a clue. Then, answer the questions that follow the paragraphs.

_____ (PON) of homeschoolers' exemption from standardized tests cite three main reasons for their views. Some parents feel that teachers are neglecting curriculums by focusing their attention on test preparation. Others point to studies that say standardized testing does not accurately reflect a student's academic performance in school. Finally, there are some who claim that standardized tests may handicap students based on gender, ethnicity, or race. While these arguments may lure some into the pro-exemption camp, the case in support of mandating testing is far more persuasive because it is based on a student's educational and social welfare.

Students in traditional school environments are supposed to believe that standardized tests are the culmination of a year of hard work and perseverance. When home-schooled children are not required to take standardized tests, many students in traditional classroom settings _____ (STRUE) their peers' exemption as meaning that school is unimportant. Tests begin to seem just another "task" without a purpose.

Lack of exposure to standardized tests places home-schooled students at a significant disadvantage. These students will eventually have to take tests for admission to college, possible job placement, and even for their driver's licenses. By neglecting to gain proper training in test-taking techniques, as well as experience with timed test formatting, they may have a difficult time proving that they are _____ (FIC) in many subject areas. Standardized tests provide an assessment of an individual in relation to a community-set norm. Without taking these tests, homeschooled students may not know what their relationship to the community truly is.

Most homeschoolers will claim that their education is equal, or even superior, to what students in public schools receive because homeschooling allows for much greater individualized instruction. Without requiring mandatory testing, though, there is no way to prove the truth of this claim. To be truly equal, or even hint at a balance, educators need some means of comparison. Standardized test results can give them the means of such analysis.

1. In the second paragraph, the author
    A. discusses the impact of exemption on students' morale.
    B. provides theories that enhance his views on standardized testing.
    C. refutes opposing arguments with statistical evidence.
    D. offers reasons that explain the failure of homeschooling.

2. With which of the following statements would the author most likely agree?
    A. Homeschooling allows students to better acquire the skills necessary for future success than traditional schooling does.
    B. The use of college admissions exams such as the SAT and ACT favors those who are schooled in traditional environments.
    C. Standardized testing is the most accurate predictor of a person's success in college.
    D. Standardized exams allow students to show their inner qualities and the traits that make them unique in society.

3. The author's point in writing this essay is to
    A. inform readers of the differences between traditional schooling and homeschooling.
    B. prove that standardized test scores are not good indications of homeschooling success.
    C. argue that no students should be required to take standardized tests.
    D. argue that homeschoolers should be required to take standardized tests.

Exercise VI. Drawing on your knowledge of roots and words in context, read the following selection and define the italicized words. If you cannot figure out the meaning of the words on your own, look them up in a dictionary. Note that *pre* means "before," and *de* means "down from."

Author Jack Proutt begins his book on *Moby-Dick* with a *preface* that offers readers the opportunity to learn the history of the novel. In the chapters that follow, Proutt uses *deconstructive* literary theory to break down the novel into its essential elements in order to gain a better understanding of the work. Critics are hailing the work as "groundbreaking," "a literary gem," and as "the most important study of Melville to hit shelves in decades."

UNIT EIGHT

PLAC
Latin PLACERE, PLACITUM, "to please"

COMPLACENT (kəm plā´ sənt) *adj.*   satisfied with a situation
L. *com*, intensifier + *placere* = too pleased
Susanna saw that the children were becoming lazy and *complacent*, so she urged them to become involved in volunteer work.
syn: pleased, unconcerned   ant: worried

PLACEBO (plə sē´ bō) *n.*   something that has a positive mental effect but no physical effect
L. literally, "I will please"
Good news on the political front is often a *placebo* for the stock market, even if it becomes bad news again the next day.

PLACID (plas´ id) *adj.*   calm; undisturbed
Tara's *placid* expression never seemed to register the chaos around her.
syn: peaceful   ant: agitated

GRAT
Latin GRATUS, "pleasing, earning thanks" or "thankful"

GRATUITOUS (grə tōō´ i təs) *adj.*   unnecessary or unwanted
L. *gratus* = *done only to please (unasked for; unneeded)*
Movies today are often criticized for *gratuitous* violence.
syn: unessential   ant: important

INGRATIATE (in grā´ shē āt) *v.*   to gain another's favor by flattery or false friendliness
L. *in*, "in, to" + *gratus* = *into favor*
Annie suspected that the student was trying to *ingratiate* himself with his teachers.

INGRATE (in´ grāt) *n.*   one who is not properly thankful
L. *in*, "not" + *gratus* = *not thankful*
When Amber threw down her birthday present in disappointment, she seemed like a spoiled little *ingrate*.

To test the effectiveness of a new medicine, a doctor may give one group of patients a placebo (sometimes called a "sugar pill"). It has no actual healing powers, but provides a control against which to test the group actually taking the medicine.

A tip is sometimes called a gratuity; it is not required, but a person grateful for a service may leave one.

DOC, DOCT
Latin DOCERE, DOCTUM, "to teach"

DOCILE (dos´ əl) *adj.* easily taught; submissive to instruction
L. *docilis,* "able to be taught"
Ruffles, who had previously been the most *docile* of the cats, suddenly started hissing and biting.
syn: obedient   *ant: defiant*

INDOCTRINATE (in dok´ tri nāt) *v.* to teach a certain point of view to
L. *in,* "into" + *docere* = *to teach into*
The cult leader attempted to *indoctrinate* his new followers in the ways of his teachings.
syn: instill

DOCTRINE (dok´ trin) *n.* that which is taught; a body of beliefs or ideas
L. *doctrina,* "a teaching"
Followers of this political *doctrine* believe that war is the solution to most political problems.
syn: creed

TEMPER
Latin TEMPERARE, TEMPERATUM, "to temper; to make less severe"

TEMPER (tem´ pər) *v.* to decrease the strength of
Serita *tempers* her spicy stew with a little milk or yogurt.

TEMPERANCE (tem´ pər ens) *n.* restraint or moderation, especially in regards to alcohol or food
Jordan's *temperance* at the buffet table spared her the indigestion that I got.
syn: frugality   *ant: indulgence*

For many, the TEMPLE was a place of TEMPERANCE.

INTEMPERATE (in tem´ pə rit) *adj.* lacking moderation; severe or extreme
L. *in,* "not" + *temperatum* = *not tempered*
In terms of climate, the Sahara Desert and Antarctica are two of the most *intemperate* places in the world.
syn: immoderate

▥ *Other synonyms for docile are* meek, mild, *and* gentle. *Other antonyms include* stubborn, mean, *and* vicious.

▥ *Be careful not to mix up the* temper *and* tempor *roots. If you see* tempor *(as in the word* temporal), *look for a meaning having to do with time.*

EXERCISES - UNIT EIGHT

Exercise I. Complete the sentence in a way that shows you understand the meaning of the italicized vocabulary word.

1.   Annie was critical of Ramon's political *doctrine* because…

2.   Harry's attempt to *ingratiate* himself with Nina actually resulted in…

3.   Because I exercised *temperance* when the first round of food and drink was served,…

4.   The *docile* mare allowed herself…

5.   Before you become *complacent* about your financial situation,…

6.   If Lloyd *tempers* his constant stream of criticism with a few positive remarks, he will find that…

7.   Although she appeared to be rather *placid* in nature, Dora…

8.   The winning lottery ticket proved to be a *placebo* for the whole town's problems, in that it…

9.   Some of the *gratuitous* luxuries in the hotel suite included…

10.   After his journey to *intemperate* North Dakota, Mel swore…

11.   The coach tried to *indoctrinate* his players with his philosophy of baseball by…

12.   Some people called the striking workers *ingrates*, but others said that…

Exercise II. Fill in the blank with the best word from the choices below. One word will not be used.

docile   complacent   temper   placebo   ingratiate

1.   My _____, good-natured little brother is a favorite of his teachers.

2.   Rather than trying to _____ herself with her new coworkers, Maxine earned their respect by doing excellent work.

3.   Lester was just beginning to grow _____ about his grades when he encountered the most difficult math test he had ever seen.

4.   Although many children find the first day of school scary, their nervousness is _____ by the excitement of new people, sights, and sounds.

Fill in the blank with the best word from the choices below. One word will not be used.

gratuitous	doctrine	placebo	placid	indoctrinate

5.   Awarding an "A" in math to everyone would only be a(n) _____ for the students; it wouldn't lead to real academic improvement.

6.   Penny didn't follow a particular religious _____ because she couldn't decide which one was right.

7.   Since he had no opponent in the election, the candidate's campaign ads seemed rather _____.

8.   If the political party cannot _____ its youngest members with its core values, how will it win the election?

Fill in the blank with the best word from the choices below. One word will not be used.

docile	ingrate	placid	temperance	intemperate

9.   I was amazed at the _____ Theo showed when faced with all kinds of temptations.

10.   Mary didn't want to seem like a(n) _____, so she graciously thanked her aunt for the sweater.

11.   The _____ expression of the moose as it stared into the window was very different from the hysterical expression of the human staring back.

12.   The _____ conditions on the top of the mountain made it difficult for anyone to survive.

Exercise III. Choose the set of words that best completes the sentence.

1.   Roberta's fiery nature was _____ by her best friend's _____ character.
   A.   ingratiated; gratuitous
   B.   indoctrinated; complacent
   C.   tempered; docile
   D.   indoctrinated; docile

2.   Darryl found that _____ luxuries tended to make him _____.
   A.   intemperate; placid
   B.   gratuitous; complacent
   C.   placid; docile
   D.   docile; complacent

3. In a naturally _____ climate, sunshine seems almost to be a(n) _____; it briefly makes everyone feel better, even though it doesn't last.
   A. placid; temperance
   B. complacent; ingrate
   C. gratuitous; ingrate
   D. intemperate; placebo

4. While one of the sisters was too _____ and would not argue even when she should have, the other was a(n) _____ who was never satisfied with any gift or kind word.
   A. gratuitous; placebo
   B. placid; ingrate
   C. complacent; doctrine
   D. intemperate; temperance

5. The _____ that Emma follows is so strict that she has to _____ the severity with amusement once in a while.
   A. placebo; indoctrinate
   B. doctrine; temper
   C. placebo; ingratiate
   D. temperance; indoctrinate

Exercise IV. Complete the sentence by inferring information about the italicized word from its context.

1. If a visitor to the company sees Frank trying to *ingratiate* himself with Mr. Leavis, he might assume that Frank wants…

2. If Doreen complains about the *intemperate* climate of the place she visited last year, Nancy can assume Doreen did not…

3. If Isaac knows that Pinky is the most *docile* rabbit in the petting zoo, he might expect the children who visit to…

Exercise V. Fill in each blank with the word from the Unit that best completes the sentence, using the root we supply as a clue. Then, answer the questions that follow the paragraphs.

Many modern media critics argue that television viewers have become increasingly _____ (PLAC) in accepting reality programs. Others deplore network executives' attempt to _____ (GRAT) themselves with viewers by presenting senseless spectacles and low-class programming. Serious dramas and lighthearted sitcoms are being shelved due to increasing costs, lack of innovation, and an inability to draw viewers away from an ever-expanding number of cable stations. To understand why reality programs have infiltrated the airwaves, however, it is important to look at the demise of traditional television programming.

Since television began, programming and costs have been its driving factors. One theory as to why this is the case states that, in order to gain a larger audience, networks must pay attention to what people want to watch. Popular programming, according to this line of thinking, attracts larger audiences, and larger audiences mean increased revenues from advertising. Television executives, therefore, need to understand that they must sell an audience what it wants, but they have been slow to do so. The networks' competition, cable, has learned this concept more rapidly than the networks themselves have.

With the spectacular growth of cable television, the once-limited spectrum of channels has become a never-ending banquet of _____ (GRAT) viewing possibilities. From music networks to food channels, news to sports, family centered programming to television for animal lovers, it seems that there are channels for everyone, no matter how small the audience. With the increased number of networks, though, come more competitors for the same number of viewers. This competition invariably leads to smaller budgets for the programs themselves. Looking to ease the pain caused by tightened budgets, cable and network programmers quickly realized that reality television shows were a means of providing a cheap and popular alternative to traditional programming.

As long as viewers flock to this type of program, both networks and cable will continue to produce them in countless numbers. The low production costs, large audiences, and rapid development of reality-based shows allow the networks to adhere to one of the fundamental _____ (DOCT) of the industry: regardless of what is good for the viewers, television will always seek to maximize its audience while minimizing its cost.

1. The main purpose of the essay is to
   A. explain why reality programming has become common on television.
   B. further the author's idea that reality programming is superior to traditional television shows.
   C. explain the cost-savings of reality programming.
   D. claim that cable television will overtake traditional television through reality shows.

2. Which of the following is the best summary of this essay?
   A. Serious dramas and lighthearted sitcoms are being shelved for their increasing costs, lack of innovation, and inability to draw viewers away from cable stations.
   B. Critics are giving viewers senseless spectacles and low-class programming.
   C. Television programming has always been a balancing act between what television viewers want and what advertisers will pay for.
   D. To understand why reality programs have infiltrated the airwaves, however, it is important to look at the demise of traditional programming.

3. The author's tone in assessing the demise of traditional programming is best described as
   A. informative.
   B. sarcastic.
   C. docile.
   D. intemperate.

Exercise VI. Drawing on your knowledge of roots and words in context, read the following selection and define the italicized words. If you cannot figure out the meaning of the words on your own, look them up in a dictionary.

The new chef at Pancake House tried hard to *placate* her sometimes-demanding customers. She spent several hours preparing food that would appeal to young and old eaters. She has been quoted as saying, "The most *gratifying* aspect of being a chef is watching people smile after a meal." Judging from the smiles on Pancake House diners, Chef Elizabeth has much to be pleased about.

UNIT NINE

TORT, TORQ
Latin TORQUERE, TORTUS, "to twist"

TORTUOUS (tôr´chōō əs) *adj.* not direct or straightforward
L. *tortus = twisting*
The *tortuous* road up the mountain was difficult and dangerous to navigate in the dark.
syn: circuitous   *ant: straightforward*

RETORT (ri tôrt´) *v.* to respond critically or sarcastically
L. *re*, "back" + *tortus = to twist (words) back*
When I complained that Paula had given me bad directions, she *retorted* that I should have used a GPS instead.
syn: reply

EXTORT (ik stôrt´) *v.* to wrongly or illegally force someone to comply with a demand
L. *ex*, "out of" + *tortus = twisted out of*
Because the corrupt official possessed potentially damaging information about his colleagues, he wanted to *extort* money from them.
syn: coerce   *ant: coax*

VOLV, VOLU
Latin VOLVERE, VOLUTUM, "to roll; to turn"

VOLUBLE (vol´yə bəl) *adj.* talkative; given to rapid, abundant speech
L. *volutum = rolling out (words)*
Our new recruit was an enthusiastic and *voluble* young man who would strike up a conversation with anyone.
syn: chatty   *ant: quiet*

CONVOLUTED (kän´və lōōt´id) *adj.* having too many twists and turns; overly complicated
L. *con*, "together" + *volutum = to roll together*
Sarah looked skeptical when she heard my *convoluted* excuse for being late.
syn: tangled   *ant: clear*

EVOLVE (ē volv´) *v.* to unfold; to develop or change gradually
L. *e*, "out of" + *volvere = to turn out*
Our volunteer group started out small, but *evolved* into a large, statewide organization.
syn: progress   *ant: regress*

Torturous means "relating to torture," while tortuous means "winding" or "twisting."

Extortion usually involves some secret threat to a person's property or reputation. Blackmail is an example of extortion.

Whereas evolution is slow and gradual change, revolution, meaning "a sudden turning over," is sudden, often violent, change.

FLEX, FLECT
Latin FLECTERE, FLECTUM, "to bend"

INFLEXIBLE   (in flĕk´ sə bəl)   *adj.*   too unchangeable in character or purpose
L. *in*, "not" + *flectum* = *not bending*
Some of Greg's students thought of him as an *inflexible* tyrant because he never allowed them extra time for assignments.
syn: *rigid, stiff*   ant: *flexible*

DEFLECT   (dē flekt´)   *v.*   to cause to turn aside or away
L. *de*, "away" + *flectum* = *to turn (something) aside*
Joe skillfully *deflected* his opponent's blows with an upraised arm.
syn: *redirect*   ant: *accept*

INFLECTION   (in flĕk´ shən)   *n.*   a change in pitch or tone of the voice
L. *in*, "in" + *flectere* = *to bend (the voice)*
If you want to make your meaning clearer, try a different *inflection* on the first words of the poem.

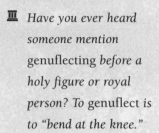

A tonsil INFECTION changed the singer's INFLECTION.

VERT, VERS
Latin VERTERE, VERSUM, "to turn"

ADVERSE   (ad vûrs´)   *adj.*   not helpful; harmful
L. *ad*, "against" + *versum* = *turned against*
We were pleased to have made it up the mountain under such *adverse* conditions.
syn: *unfortunate, injurious*   ant: *conducive*

REVERT   (ri vûrt´)   *v.*   to fall back into an old condition
L. *re*, "back" + *vertere* = *to turn (something) back*
Annie hopes never to *revert* to the bad habits she gave up.
syn: *lapse*   ant: *improve*

SUBVERT   (səb vûrt´)   *v.*   to undermine; to corrupt
L. *sub*, "beneath" + *vertere* = *to turn from beneath*
The queen was afraid the rebellious subjects would *subvert* her authority.
syn: *invalidate*   ant: *support*

Have you ever heard someone mention genuflecting *before a holy figure or royal person? To genuflect is to "bend at the knee."*

How do the words reflect *and* inflect *show their Latin origins?*

I didn't like the play, but then I saw it under adverse *conditions— the curtain was up.*
—Groucho Marx, 20th-century American comedian

EXERCISES - UNIT NINE

Exercise I. Complete the sentence in a way that shows you understand the meaning of the italicized vocabulary word.

1. A clear sign that the author's poems had *evolved* was…

2. In an attempt to *extort* money from the businessmen in his district, the councilman…

3. The manager who was caught stealing tried to *deflect* blame by…

4. When the rebel leader tried to *subvert* the authority of the military government,…

5. The author employed some peculiar *inflections* while lecturing, leading the audience to…

6. When the interviewer accused the singer of being a drama queen, the singer *retorted* that…

7. Some of the *adverse* circumstances facing the young violinist were…

8. During the *tortuous* journey along the winding, overgrown mountain path…

9. Although known as an *inflexible* interpreter of the Constitution, the Supreme Court justice…

10. I found the film's central plot so *convoluted* and difficult to follow that…

11. The children who had gathered on our front porch were so *voluble* that…

12. Sharon *reverted* to some of her old patterns of eating because…

Exercise II. Fill in the blank with the best word from the choices below. One word will not be used.

revert	voluble	adverse	extort	evolve

1. With the help of my friends, I not only got through a(n) _____ situation, but I also learned from it.

2. When the new computer system crashed because of a virus, we had to temporarily _____ to an old one.

3. Rather than using the appropriate legal channels, Sid tried to _____ information from members of the city council.

4. One of the more _____ teachers kept talking even after the bell rang, and his students were forced to stay and listen.

Fill in the blank with the best word from the choices below. One word will not be used.

deflect   inflexible   evolve   retort   tortuous

5. The audience had the pleasure of watching a good opera _____ into a truly spectacular one.

6. I try to be open-minded rather than _____ when it comes to the subject of love.

7. A quick, sarcastic _____ silenced the journalist who had asked an inappropriate question.

8. Our small, agile boat could easily navigate the _____ curves of the river.

Fill in the blank with the best word from the choices below. One word will not be used.

deflect   adverse   inflection   convoluted   subvert

9. By varying the _____ on a particular word or note, a singer can bring many different meanings out of the same song.

10. The reasoning behind the budget disaster was so _____ that no one could begin to untangle it.

11. In an attempt to _____ the election results, the politician threw away several boxes of ballots.

12. You will not always be able to _____ criticism away from yourself.

Exercise III. Choose the set of words that best completes the sentence.

1. When you find yourself facing _____ circumstances, will you be able to adapt, or will you be _____?
   A. convoluted; tortuous
   B. adverse; voluble
   C. adverse; inflexible
   D. inflexible; convoluted

2. On some days Nicki felt she was _____ into a mature, graceful person, but on others she _____ to her old, bad habits.
   A. evolving; deflected
   B. deflecting; subverted
   C. evolving; reverted
   D. extorting; evolved

3. In an attempt to _____ the power of the ruling party, the corrupt official tried to _____ money from the vice president.
    A. retort; revert
    B. evolve; retort
    C. subvert; extort
    D. retort; deflect

4. I could barely stand to listen to Kim recite the poem; almost every _____ seemed wrong to me, and I found the poem _____ and confusing anyway.
    A. inflection; inflexible
    B. retort; voluble
    C. inflection; convoluted
    D. retort; adverse

5. When I teased Marge for being stern and _____, her _____ was that I would go along with anyone.
    A. tortuous; inflection
    B. adverse; retort
    C. voluble; inflection
    D. inflexible; retort

Exercise IV. Complete the sentence by inferring information about the italicized word from its context.

1. If a group of citizens tries to *subvert* the influence of a large corporation, the citizens probably feel that the corporation…

2. If Larry says that Carl tried to *extort* information from him, we can assume that Larry…

3. If Kathy says that she has *reverted* to her smoking habit in the month of December, in November she probably…

Exercise V. Fill in each blank with the word from the Unit that best completes the sentence, using the root we supply as a clue. Then, answer the questions that follow the paragraphs.

"Just because something doesn't do what you planned it to do in the first place doesn't mean it's useless…Surprises and reverses should be an incentive to great accomplishment." This quote from Thomas Alva Edison applies nicely to his own life and work. Had he been more _____ (FLEX), he could never have adjusted to the countless instances of rejection that preceded his enormous and important successes. Edison's determination to adapt to anything he deemed a challenge profited the world in ways few people could imagine at the time.

Edison's fierce resolve developed partly in reaction to _____ (VERS) circumstances. At age fourteen, he contracted scarlet fever, which robbed him of all the hearing in his left ear and 80 percent in the right. For the rest of his life, he would be driven to understand and solve the problems people face in dealing with their environments. Fortunately, he had enough foresight to understand the importance of the whole problem-solving process. "If I find 10,000 ways something won't work, I haven't failed," he said. "I am not discouraged because every wrong attempt discarded is just one more step forward."

As he became an adult, Edison's youthful optimism _____ (VOLV) into a powerful drive to succeed. During the quiet hours of his job at Western Union, he worked feverishly on an electronic voting machine and applied for his first patent. The Massachusetts Legislature rejected the invention, leaving him with a beautifully designed machine that could not be marketed. Consequently, Edison vowed to "never waste time inventing things that people would not want to buy." However, this vow did not stop him from conducting experiments that were not certain to succeed. He later viewed his 500 to 600 abandoned patent applications as homework.

In 1869, a corporation paid Edison $40,000 for the rights to his stock-ticker, which set him on a trail of creating successful inventions for industrial use. At age 29, he invented the carbon transmitter, which ultimately led to devices like the telephone and the phonograph. The first incandescent electric light bulb, a centrally generating and distributing electric power system, and the first silent motion picture soon followed. By the 1920s, Edison was producing defensive devices for submarines and ships and many useful inventions related to rubber, concrete, and ethanol. Edison eventually patented over 1,000 inventions in his desire to benefit mankind.

"I never perfected an invention that I did not think about in terms of the service it might give others," he once said. "I find out what the world needs, then I proceed to invent." Without Edison's perseverance and spirit of service, many advances in technology would have been delayed by many years.

1. What did Edison mean when he said, "If I find 10,000 ways something won't work, I haven't failed"?
    A. Failure in an experiment can be a kind of success.
    B. Failures come when something will not work.
    C. Success is profitable.
    D. Success comes only when something will not work.

2. According to the passage, which of the following would Edison probably consider a failure?
    A. a rejected patent application
    B. lack of education
    C. giving up on an invention
    D. a financial disaster

3. According to the passage, which of the following was NOT one of Edison's successful inventions?
    A. electric light
    B. stock-ticker
    C. silent movie
    D. voting machine

Exercise VI. Drawing on your knowledge of roots and words in context, read the following selection and define the italicized words. If you cannot figure out the meaning of the words on your own, look them up in a dictionary. Note that the prefix *in* means "not."

The *voluminous* works of famous author Charles Dickens fill an entire bookshelf. The countless novels, short stories, and other writings have kept literary scholars busy for years studying the Victorian themes that Dickens explored. One scholar, Harvey Forrester, was lucky enough to *inadvertently* find a connection between Dickens and one of his most famous characters—Oliver Twist. Forrester noticed that Dickens and Twist both shared a passion for travel and adventure. For Forrester, the find was career defining.

UNIT TEN

CRIMIN
Latin CRIMEN, "crime, charge of crime"

DECRIMINALIZE   (dē krim´ ən əl īz)   v.   to do away with legal penalties for
L. *de*, "away, off" + *crimen* = (to take) a crime away
Eric is part of a group that is calling upon the government to *decriminalize* certain drugs.

INCRIMINATE   (in krim´ ə nāt)   v.   to reveal guilt or make (someone) appear
   guilty
L. *in*, "onto" + *crimen* = to (put) crime onto
If the stolen necklace we found in your drawer doesn't *incriminate* you, I don't know what does.
syn: implicate   *ant: acquit*

RECRIMINATION   (rē krim´ ə nā shən)   n.   an accusation made in reply; a
   counter charge
L. *re*, "back" + *crimen* = a charge (made) back
The two friends got into a bitter fight and began hurling *recriminations* at one another.
syn: rebuke

CULP
Latin CULPARE, CULPATUM, "to blame"

CULPABLE   (kul´ pə bəl)   adj.   deserving blame
L. *culpatum* + *able* = able to be blamed
Marshall, who ran the Tilt-a-Whirl, considered himself *culpable* for the accident at the amusement park.
syn: liable   *ant: blameless*

CULPRIT   (kul´ prit)   n.   one responsible for a crime
Police currently have no idea who the *culprit* behind the fire might be, but they have a long list of suspects.
syn: perpetrator

MEA CULPA   (mā´ ə   kul´ pə)   interjection   a statement uttered to show
   personal responsibility for a wrong
Directly from Latin *mea culpa*, "my fault"
"*Mea culpa!*" said Miguela, with some embarrassment, when she realized that she'd left the car windows down.

The 5th Amendment to the US Constitution serves as a protection against self-incrimination, meaning that people, even if guilty, cannot be forced to testify in court against themselves. This right, even though it is not part of the amendment, extends to husbands and wives, who cannot be forced to give information that might incriminate a spouse.

Crimes against the innocent will not stop until the victim is not made to feel like the culprit. —Anonymous

ONUS, ONER
Latin ONUS, "burden"

ONUS (ō´ nəs) *n.* a burden or obligation
The *onus* of proving that this man was at the crime scene now rests on the detective.
syn: duty

ONEROUS (on´ ər əs) *adj.* unpleasant and burdensome
Dr. Lassiter faced the *onerous* task of telling the patient that his cancer had spread.
syn: demanding   *ant: easy*

EXONERATE (ig zon´ ə rāt) *v.* to prove not guilty
L. *ex*, "out of" + *onus* = *out of the burden (of proof)*
We feel sure the evidence we have uncovered will *exonerate* Anna.
syn: acquit   *ant: condemn, convict*

Since nobody else would do it, the ONUS of moving the piano was ON US.

PROB, PROV
Latin PROBARE, PROBATUM, "to prove good; to approve"

APPROBATION (ap rə bā´ shən) *n.* praise or approval
L. *ad*, "toward" + *probare* = *to take approval toward*
Ellen won widespread *approbation* for her work in biomedical research.
syn: commendation   *ant: condemnation*

REPROBATE (rep´ rə bāt) *n.* a dishonest or immoral person; a scoundrel
L. *re*, "back, away from" + *probare* = *one away from approval*
The *reprobates* who set fire to the forest must be caught and punished.
syn: delinquent

REPROVE (ri prōōv´) *v.* to scold or criticize
L. *re*, "back" + *probare* = *approval back*
My aunt Thelma gently *reproved* me for taking more than my share of dessert.
syn: chide   *ant: praise*

▥ Onus *is usually used in legal settings; the onus probandi, or "burden of proof," is that which a person must convince a judge or jury to believe.*

▥ *The Latin* probare *means "to test" and "to test something for goodness." We get both* prove *and* approve *from this verb.*

EXERCISES - UNIT TEN

Exercise I. Complete the sentence in a way that shows you understand the meaning of the italicized vocabulary word.

1. When Jed called out "*Mea culpa!*" in response to the malfunction of the copier, we knew that...

2. The police will catch the *culprit* behind the wave of vandalism by...

3. The other members of the political party showed their *approbation* of the idea by...

4. Even though all the evidence seems to *incriminate* Mr. Dawson,...

5. When I was younger, I had a reputation for being somewhat of a *reprobate* because...

6. Rather than *exonerating* the driver of the car, the footage from the traffic camera...

7. Before something can be *decriminalized*, it...

8. When Ray *reproved* Caroline for leaving the toys on the stairs, she...

9. The most *onerous* job a farmer of today has to do is probably...

10. Because I consider myself *culpable* for the boat accident, I will...

11. The *onus* of proving that a dog is not dangerous should be borne by...

12. As the two men exchanged *recriminations*, their friends...

Exercise II. Fill in the blank with the best word from the choices below. One word will not be used.

exonerate   reprove   culprit   onerous   approbation

1. When Josie's mother _____ her for coming home late, Josie hung her head in shame.

2. I was given the _____ job of dealing with a huge crowd of impatient and complaining customers.

3. The _____ in the cookie theft is probably between three and six years old.

4. The defendant's lawyers hope the new testimony will _____ their client.

Fill in the blank with the best word from the choices below. One word will not be used.

reprove	recrimination	reprobate	approbation	decriminalize

5. Some people argue that the US should completely _____ attempted suicide, but psychiatrists claim that may lead to more deaths.

6. The principal felt that the boys were habitual _____ and should be expelled from school.

7. Jesse refused to state publicly what _____ he had included in the angry letter to his boss.

8. The _____ of the judges' panel meant a lot to the nervous young dancer.

Fill in the blank with the best word from the choices below. One word will not be used.

onus	incriminate	mea culpa	culpable	reprobate

9. Just being present when an accident occurs doesn't make you _____ for that accident.

10. Philip now carries the _____ of defending his brother's good character.

11. My father said that my guilty expression _____ me more than anything else.

12. When I saw that my actions had caused a fight between my friends, I thought to myself, "_____."

Exercise III. Choose the set of words that best completes the sentence.

1. The young man accused of the crime may have a reputation for being a(n) _____, but reputation alone is not enough to _____ him.
   A. reprobate; decriminalize
   B. reprobate; incriminate
   C. onus; reprove
   D. culprit; decriminalize

2. By expressing _____ when you should _____ instead, you are sending a message that bad behavior is acceptable.
   A. recrimination; incriminate
   B. approbation; decriminalize
   C. approbation; reprove
   D. onus; incriminate

3.	The _____ of proving that the man is not the _____ who committed the crime falls on his team of lawyers.
	A.	onus; culprit
	B.	onus; approbation
	C.	culprit; recrimination
	D.	culprit; onus

4.	If the city council should choose to _____ speeding, it would be _____ for any injury received as a result of it.
	A.	reprove; onerous
	B.	decriminalize; culpable
	C.	incriminate; exonerated
	D.	exonerate; onerous

5.	Patrick felt that if he could _____ Francine of the charge against her, he would earn her _____ and respect.
	A.	exonerate; approbation
	B.	incriminate; culprit
	C.	reprove; reprobate
	D.	reprove; approbation

Exercise IV. Complete the sentence by inferring information about the italicized word from its context.

1.	If someone passing by a rally notices that a speaker has earned the *approbation* of his listeners, the passerby might assume…

2.	If a voter who knows nothing about two political figures hears them trading *recriminations*, the voter might guess the two figures are…

3.	When an investigation concludes that one driver in a two-car wreck is not *culpable*, the police will probably say that…

Exercise V. Fill in each blank with the word from the Unit that best completes the sentence, using the root we supply as a clue. Then, answer the questions that follow the paragraphs.

Americans like to think that under our system of justice, _____ (CULP) are brought to trial, convicted, and punished. Yet, the system is not perfect, and, at times, in the presence of supposedly _____ (CRIMIN) evidence, innocent people are swept up and wrongly convicted.

The science of DNA testing has been a major factor in changing the criminal justice system and determining responsibility for crimes. Supporters of such testing feel that it has provided scientific proof that our system routinely convicts and sentences innocent people, and that wrongful convictions are not the isolated or rare events they were once thought to be. Most important, DNA testing has opened a window into wrongful convictions so that the causes of such mistakes can be studied and remedies proposed.

Unfortunately, because of the _____ (ONER) expense of mounting a scientific defense, many people who could benefit from DNA testing have not had access to it. Part of the growing movement to reform the criminal justice system involves correcting such irregularities in the availability of technology. As an example, consider the Innocence Project at the Benjamin N. Cardozo School of Law.

The Innocence Project was set up as a nonprofit legal clinic, and it handles only cases in which DNA testing may yield conclusive proof of guilt or innocence. At the clinic, students, overseen by a team of attorneys and staff, handle the casework. Clients of the Project are generally people with very limited resources who have used up all of their other legal options. Many, it turns out, have been convicted on the grounds of mistaken identity or coerced confessions. Often, their last hope is that biological evidence from a case still exists for DNA testing.

Over the years, the Innocence Project has become more than a "court of last resort" for inmates who have exhausted their appeals and financial resources. The Project now helps law schools, journalism schools, and public defense offices across the country in proving the innocence of the wrongly convicted. To date, more than 330 people have been _____ (ONER) through the work of the Innocence Project staff.

Because human beings, who inevitably make mistakes, govern US courts, the probability of wrongful conviction in criminal cases will likely never be eliminated. However, as advancing science and technology take more and more of the guesswork out of investigations, unjust and erroneous verdicts will become more infrequent occurrences—so long as such technologies are within reach of all who need them.

1. Why does the author bring up the Innocence Project?
   A. as a way of explaining the beginnings of DNA testing
   B. to give an example of a trend in providing fair access to technology
   C. to give an example of the movement to reform wrongly convicted defendants
   D. as a way of showing defendants' access to technology

2. Which statement contradicts material found in the passage?
   A. The Innocence Project uses modern technology, students, and public defenders in its work.
   B. DNA testing can be a last chance for some inmates who have tried other legal methods.
   C. The Innocence Project collects money from the state after it frees a prisoner through DNA.
   D. Over 300 people have been freed through work that the Innocence Project has conducted.

3. What is the purpose of the third paragraph?
   A. to explain why DNA testing is gaining supporters
   B. to warn that the courts will always make mistakes
   C. to explain why testing is not always available
   D. to show who might benefit from DNA testing

4. Judging by this paragraph, what would earn the approval of the Innocence Project staff?
   A. the government's establishment of a large fund for DNA testing
   B. the advancement of DNA technology beyond the power of the court
   C. the allocation of financial resources to traditional investigating techniques
   D. the conviction of a person based on DNA testing

Exercise VI. Drawing on your knowledge of roots and words in context, read the following selection and define the italicized words. If you cannot figure out the meaning of the words on your own, look them up in a dictionary. Note that the prefix in means "into, against."

The primary goal of the District Attorney was to convince the jury to *inculpate* the defendant in the murder trial. In order to do this, the D.A. presented the results of the *probe* into the defendant's whereabouts on the day of the murder. Since this investigation did place the defendant away from the crime scene, the D.A. dropped all charges.

UNIT ELEVEN

FID
Latin FIDERE, FISUS, "to trust; to believe"

DIFFIDENT (dif´ i dənt) *adj.* shy; not assertive
L. *dis*, "not" + *fidere* = *not trusting*
The young student, fearing the wrath of her teacher, spoke in a quiet, *diffident* voice.
syn: *bashful*   ant: *confident*

FIDELITY (fəd el´ ə tē) *n.* faithfulness; loyalty
L. *fidelis*, "faithfulness" from *fidere*
The *fidelity* shown by the soldier was the subject of a book and a film.
ant: *treachery*

CONFIDE (kən fīd´) *v.* to trust (another) with information or a secret
L. *con*, "with" + *fidere* = *to be trusting with*
Gerri *confided* to me that she was very nervous about performing for the first time.
ant: *conceal*

FALL
Latin FALLERE, FALSUM, "to deceive"

FALLACY (fal´ ə sē) *n.* a misleading or mistaken idea
L. *fallax*, "deceptive (idea)" from *fallere*
Even if I could convince myself that everyone feels the way I do, I would know in my heart that it was a *fallacy*.
syn: *misconception*   ant: *truth*

FALLACIOUS (fə lā´ shəs) *adj.* misleading or deceptive
The council accused the businessman of unethical conduct and *fallacious* wording of contracts.

FALLIBLE (fal´ ə bəl) *adj.* capable of being mistaken; imperfect
fallere + *ible*, "able to be" = *able to be deceived*
My brother strongly believed in the cause, but he was as *fallible* as any human being, and temptation led him astray.
ant: *infallible, flawless*

The official motto of the United States Marine Corps is "Semper Fidelis," which means "always faithful."

We get the word fail *from* fallere.

If your computer works fine until you put in a USB flash drive, and it crashes the next day, it is a logical fallacy, *called "post hoc, ergo propter hoc," to assume the flash drive caused the crash.*

CRED
Latin CREDERE, CREDITUM, "to trust; to believe"

CREDIBLE (kred´i bəl) *adj.* able to be trusted in
    or believed
L. *credere + ible*, "able to be" = *able to be believed*
Sam's story about the avalanche was amazing but
credible.
syn: valid   *ant: doubtful*

Although Sam told me that tires are *EDIBLE*, something tells me that isn't *CREDIBLE*.

CREDENCE (krē´dəns) *n.* a trust or belief
I did not give *credence* to the rumors about the sheriff.
syn: acceptance   *ant: mistrust*

CREDULITY (krə jōō´li tē) *n.* a tendency to believe things too quickly or easily
As Gabrielle grew older, she lost her innocent *credulity* and became more cynical
about people's intentions.
syn: gullibility   *ant: skepticism*

INCREDULOUS (in krej´ə ləs) *adj.* unable to believe something; amazed
L. *in*, "not" + *credere* = *not believing*
When Pete heard what I said, he gave me an *incredulous* stare.
syn: skeptical   *ant: trusting*

DUB
Latin DUBIUS, "doubtful"
Latin DUBITARE, DUBITATUM, "to doubt"

DUBIOUS (dōō´bē əs) *adj.* uncertain; doubtful
Penny seemed rather *dubious* about the whole idea of skydiving.
syn: unconvinced   *ant: positive*

INDUBITABLE (in dōō´bi tə bəl) *adj.* certain beyond doubt or question
L. *in*, "not" + *dubius* = *not able to be doubted*
The mechanic was a man of *indubitable* loyalty.
syn: absolute   *ant: unsure*

REDOUBTABLE (rē dout´ə bəl) *adj.* worthy of fear or respect; mighty
Middle French *redouter*, "dread" (from L. *re*, "again" + *dubius*, "doubt")
Even the most *redoubtable* of the warriors did not last very long in the blizzard.
syn: formidable

Ⅲ *Many people have little credence in provable scientific facts, which leaves them open to conspiracy theories such as believing that UFOs and Sasquatch are real, that the moon landing was staged, and that 9/11 was a plot to seize Middle East oil.*

Ⅲ Doubt *also comes from* dubitare. *If you have trouble remembering the meaning of* redoubtable, *just think of something so powerful that it makes you doubt yourself again and again.*

EXERCISES - UNIT ELEVEN

Exercise I. Complete the sentence in a way that shows you understand the meaning of the italicized vocabulary word.

1. Because of the *credence* the townspeople gave to the stories of witchcraft, they…

2. When I said that her argument constituted a logical *fallacy*, Mariah responded that…

3. One thing that made George painfully aware of how *fallible* he really could be was…

4. Although Risa has developed a *credible* theory about weather patterns,…

5. Because of the *credulity* Fiona displayed when her peers told her made-up stories, they…

6. The *fallacious* reasoning in the essay on American politics might lead the reader to…

7. When the doctor noticed his patient looking *dubious* about the surgery, he…

8. Leon's *fidelity* and trustworthiness when it came to minding the company's finances made him…

9. Only the most *redoubtable* athletes are able to…

10. Because Louisa's classmates considered her rather *diffident*, they often…

11. If I *confide* in you regarding the major new plan to restructure the city, I expect you to…

12. It is *indubitable* that the world will experience…

13. Veronica was *incredulous* at the sight of the volcano because…

Exercise II. Fill in the blank with the best word from the choices below. One word will not be used.

fidelity   redoubtable   dubious   confide   diffident

1. Although she looked _____ when I suggested climbing the fence, Lizzie went along with the plan.

2. The _____ you displayed when your friends were in danger shows me how loyal you really are.

3. I hope that Andrew will not _____ in Jeff since Jeff has a reputation for spreading other people's secrets around.

4. The army was facing its most _____ foe, a force almost three times bigger than itself.

Fill in the blank with the best word from the choices below. One word will not be used.

| fallacy | diffident | fallacious | credulity | indubitable |

5.   That the evidence was falsified now seems _____.

6.   Dr. Leary's more _____ patients are sometimes too shy or nervous to ask questions about their health.

7.   The _____ that you showed to the car salesman will make him think he can overcharge you.

8.   Do not try to undermine my argument with _____ logic and unreliable evidence.

Fill in the blank with the best word from the choices below. One word will not be used.

| fallible | credible | credence | dubious | fallacy | incredulous |

9.   The detective thought the witness's story was _____ enough.

10.   Until I fell in love with someone who was totally uninterested in me, I really didn't think I was _____.

11.   How much _____ do you give to the flashy stories you see on the local news?

12.   Although the salesman's pitch was convincing, it was based on a(n) _____.

13.   My grandmother is over 80, and many of my friends are _____ that she still plays tennis.

Exercise III. Choose the set of words that best completes the sentence.

1.   Although he was quiet, even _____, in school, Vince became a(n) _____ warrior on the football field.
      A. fallacious; incredulous
      B. indubitable; dubious
      C. diffident; redoubtable
      D. fallible; indubitable

2.   Although some of the group found the story _____, other members were highly _____ about it.
      A. diffident; credible
      B. redoubtable; fallacious
      C. incredulous; fallible
      D. credible; dubious

3.   Henry knew that he was _____, but he looked _____ when he heard about the mistake he had made.
      A. redoubtable; fallible
      B. fallacious; diffident
      C. credible; diffident
      D. fallible; incredulous

4.   When Mary _____ in me that she was a millionaire, I wondered if she was testing my _____.
      A. confided; diffidence
      B. confided; fallacy
      C. confided; credulity
      D. confided; fidelity

5.   Even though the secret agent was acquitted of spying on his own country, people he worked with
      thought he was of _____ _____, and few in the agency ever trusted him again.
      A. fallacious; credulity
      B. dubious; fidelity
      C. credible; fallacy
      D. redoubtable; credulity

Exercise IV. Complete the sentence by inferring information about the italicized word from its context.

1.   If Norman looks *incredulous* when he hears about his salary raise, we can infer that his raise is…

2.   When a reviewer says that a play's magnificence is *indubitable*, he probably believes that…

3.   If a farmer refuses to give *credence* to a report about livestock illness, he might be assuming that…

**Exercise V. Fill in each blank with the word from the Unit that best completes the sentence, using the root
      we supply as a clue. Then, answer the questions that follow the paragraphs.**

Since President Richard Nixon resigned in shame from office in 1974, the American public has generally held the opinion that elected officials are _____ (FALL). This was a common enough opinion before Nixon, but it was the Watergate Scandal that really affected all of Nixon's successors and made voters understand that presidents were, first and foremost, politicians. After Watergate, presidents' solemn oath to "preserve, protect, and defend the Constitution of the United States" sounded like little more than an empty repetition of a vow. Commanders in Chief seemed to be primarily in the service of their own interests and agenda, rather than the service of the citizens whom they represented.

Presidents are expected to exhibit a high level of _____ (FID) to the American people, as well as to the Constitution. Accordingly, they must monitor all of their own actions, both public and private, with the utmost scrutiny. In Nixon's case, several high-level officials of his administration were directly involved in an attempt to obtain information illegally from Nixon's Democratic opponents. The material the burglars collected was to be used in Nixon's upcoming reelection campaign. The scheme was exposed when a night watchman became aware of a burglary at the Watergate Hotel, where the Democratic National Committee had its headquarters. To compound matters, Nixon, attempting to conceal his own administration's involvement in the burglary, instigated a massive cover-up of the facts.

Nixon was formally impeached, but before the Senate could remove him from office, he resigned. The idea that the highest-ranking elected representative of the American people could be involved in something as obviously criminal as breaking-and-entering was severely damaging to the trust Americans had for all elected officials. Succeeding presidents attempted to win back the favor and faith of their populace, but generally wound up losing their good reputations in one scandal after another. Ronald Reagan, for instance, was deeply involved in the Iran-Contra Scandal; Bill Clinton was continually investigated for financial misdeeds and personal misconduct.

Many Americans surveyed in the years since Richard Nixon's resignation have admitted that they do not find many of the White House's promises _____ (CRED); in fact, surveys show that most citizens are _____ (DUB) about the honesty of elected officials in general. Such is the unfortunate legacy of the Watergate Scandal.

1.   Which sentence below best sums up a main idea of the passage?
      A. The American people are skeptical of politicians by nature.
      B. The American people are cynical as a result of experience.
      C. The American people are troubled by the idea of elected officials.
      D. The American people repeatedly betray their politicians.

2.   What is the Watergate Scandal?
      A. the hotel that President Richard Nixon's men broke into
      B. the burglary that was the cause of Nixon's resignation
      C. where the Democratic National Committee headquarters was
      D. another name for President Ronald Reagan's Iran-Contra Scandal

3.   Which of the following was a side effect of the Watergate Scandal?
      A. Democrats ceased trusting in any Republican official.
      B. American voters began to have negative feelings about earlier presidents.
      C. Succeeding elected officials did not have the trust of the American people.
      D. A night watchman discovered a burglary at the Watergate Hotel.

Exercise VI. Drawing on your knowledge of roots and words in context, read the following selection and define the italicized words. If you cannot figure out the meaning of the words on your own, look them up in a dictionary. Note that the prefix *ac* (from *ad*) means "toward" and the prefix *in* means "not."

During the Protestant Reformation, many Christians deserted the Catholic Church. Growing distrust of the Church led these men and women to branch off and start their own sects. The Pope, though, did not *accredit* these sects. Because the Protestants did not have the approval of the Pope, many Catholics considered them *infidels*.

UNIT TWELVE

ULTIMA
Latin ULTIMUS, "last"

ULTIMATE (ul´ tə mət) *adj.*   surpassing all others; definitive
L. *ultimus = having a final quality*
The *ultimate* humiliation came when Robbie's teacher yelled at him in front of the whole class.

PENULTIMATE (pen ul´ tə mət) *adj.*   just before the final; next-to-last
L. *paene*, "almost" + *ultimus = the next to last*
In the *penultimate* chapter of the book, the author prepares us for the shocking twists of the final chapter.

ULTIMATUM (ul tə māt´ əm) *n.*   a demand or threat that is final
L. *ultimus = (that which is) final*
The pirates gave us an *ultimatum*: either reveal where the prisoners were or walk the plank.

FIN
Latin FINIS, "end, border, limit"

INFINITE (in´ fə nit) *adj.*   without beginning or end
L. *in*, "not" + *finis = (having) no end*
Although Seth was a man of seemingly *infinite* patience, he sometimes became frustrated.

DEFINITIVE (dē fin´ ə tiv) *adj.*   defining for all others; standard
L. *de*, "from" + *finis = (measurable) from its limits*
John did not consider the work a *definitive* authority on the history of tennis.
syn: *absolute*   ant: *uncertain*

INFINITESIMAL (in fin i tes´ ə məl) *adj.*   extremely small; incalculably or
     immeasurably small
L. *in*, "not" + *finis = (so small as to have) no measure*
If any of the contaminant is left in the water supply, it is there only in *infinitesimal* amounts.
syn: *microscopic*   ant: *huge*

The ultima of a word is its final syllable; the penultima is the next-to-last syllable.

When a child is growing up, parents shouldn't give an ultimatum that they are not willing to enforce. The child never learns consequences under those circumstances.

As many atoms exist in a grain of sand as there are grains of sand on a medium-sized beach, yet that number, even if you include all the beaches in the world, is not infinite. The idea of infinity is very difficult to grasp—something continuing or extending forever, without end.

NOV
Latin NOVUS, "new"

NOVEL (näv´ əl) *adj.* new and different
The company had a *novel* approach to the problem of engine breakdown.
syn: original   *ant: stale*

NOVICE (näv´ is) *n.* an inexperienced person; an
    amateur
L. *novitia*, "one who is new" from *novus*
Even I, a chess *novice*, could appreciate the beauty of the master's play.
syn: beginner   *ant: expert*

The NOVICE gangster had
"NO VICE" yet.

INNOVATIVE (in ə vā´ tiv) *adj.* showing creativity and originality
L. *in*, intensifier + *novus* = *very new*
The *innovative* design of the new C-267 makes it the easiest vacuum cleaner to use.
syn: inventive   *ant: conservative*

PRIM
Latin PRIMUS, "first"

PRIMAL (prī´ məl) *adj.* original; dating from the beginning of existence
Fear is one of our more *primal* emotions; it helped our ancient ancestors survive.
syn: primitive   *ant: modern*

PRIMEVAL (prī mē´vəl) *adj.* extremely ancient; of earliest time
L. *primus* + *aevum*, "age" = *(dating from) the first age*
The rough cliffs had a *primeval* splendor that made us think of the beginning of time.
syn: primordial

PRIMACY (prī´ mə sē) *n.* the condition of being first in time or importance
No one in the precinct dared question the *primacy* of the police captain.

▥ *In literature the ambition of the* novice *is to acquire the literary language: the struggle of the adept is to get rid of it.* —George Bernard Shaw, 19th- 20th-century British playwright.

▥ *Many settings for novels take place in* primeval *jungles and forests before civilization arrived.* Tarzan, The Last of the Mohicans, Lord of the Flies, *and most of* The Lord of the Rings *trilogy take place in this type of environment.*

EXERCISES - UNIT TWELVE

Exercise I. Complete the sentence in a way that shows you understand the meaning of the italicized vocabulary word.

1.   Corey considered losing the class presidency the *ultimate* regret of his life, since he…

2.   Emotions like fear and hatred are often referred to as *primal* because…

3.   When the advertisement claimed that the design of the computer was *novel*,…

4.   Because Maria started to believe that her father's financial resources were *infinite*,…

5.   The *primeval* beauty of the ancient forest reminded Sharon that…

6.   When our manager heard some of the *innovative* ideas we had come up with, he…

7.   If the workers who are on strike do not follow their employer's *ultimatum*…

8.   As a *novice* on the ski slopes, I often…

9.   Because the students were in only the *penultimate* rehearsal for the play, they…

10.   Mr. Wendal became the *definitive* expert on whales and dolphins by…

11.   Members of the rebel army started to question the *primacy* of their leader because…

12.   The amount of water on the foreign planet was *infinitesimal*, and the explorers…

Exercise II. Fill in the blank with the best word from the choices below. One word will not be used.

   novel   infinite   penultimate   primal   infinitesimal

1.   The microscope was so powerful that it allowed us to see things of an almost _____ size.

2.   The _____ surprise came when we found our dog was going to have puppies, but the final shock was that our cat was going to have kittens at the same time.

3.   I felt a surge of raw, _____ anger when I saw that my house had been destroyed.

4.   Many astronomers argue over whether the universe is _____ or has limits.

Fill in the blank with the best word from the choices below. One word will not be used.

  novice   infinite   primacy   novel   ultimatum

5.   Percy still needs help with his free throws because he is a basketball _____.

6.   The general issued a(n) _____ to the enemy soldiers: they could lay down their weapons or be fired upon.

7.   The preacher warned that the _____ of spiritual laws cannot be forgotten, even when day-to-day life becomes difficult.

8.   One _____ solution to the arguments that broke out at every meeting was to give each club member a speaking time in advance.

Fill in the blank with the best word from the choices below. One word will not be used.

  innovative   definitive   ultimate   primeval   penultimate

9.   Because Julio is so shy, public speaking seems like the _____ torture to him.

10.   The _____ book on how to make pizza was written by a man who owned a pizza parlor for many years.

11.   One of the most _____ uses of technology that I saw at the computer showcase was a program that helps blind children learn to read.

12.   The statue in the museum was a representation of a(n) _____ god of fire.

Exercise III. Choose the set of words that best completes the sentence.

1.   The _____ of freedom of religion in the minds of the people was clear when they issued a(n) _____ to the tyrant.
   A.   novice; ultimatum
   B.   ultimatum; novice
   C.   primacy; ultimatum
   D.   primacy; novice

2.   One of the most _____ features of the new motor was that, unlike the old model, it released only_____ amounts of harmful chemicals.
   A.   novel; infinitesimal
   B.   definitive; penultimate
   C.   primeval; novel
   D.   primeval; definitive

3. The psychologist has written the _____ work on _____ emotions like fear, hate, and desire.
    A. primeval; novel
    B. penultimate; ultimate
    C. novel; infinitesimal
    D. definitive; primal

4. As a(n) _____ in swimming, I was given the _____ thrill when I got to meet an Olympic swimming champion.
    A. ultimatum; definitive
    B. novice; ultimate
    C. ultimatum; primeval
    D. novice; primeval

5. I was amazed at some of the _____ tools the ancient people had used in their _____ surroundings.
    A. primeval; definitive
    B. innovative; primeval
    C. ultimate; definitive
    D. novel; penultimate

Exercise IV. Complete the sentence by inferring information about the italicized word from its context.

1. If Regan hears someone on the television describing *primeval* hunters, she will probably think of...

2. Charles is upset because he lost to a *novice* chess player, and he probably believes that...

3. If a noted history scholar calls a particular research paper *definitive*, she is probably recommending that...

Exercise V. Fill in each blank with the word from the Unit that best completes the sentence, using the root we supply as a clue. Then, answer the questions that follow the paragraphs.

Albert Schweitzer, noted scholar, musician, doctor, and humanitarian, felt that his life was directed by divine calling. Even his many secular interests seem to have been colored by religious yearning. His numerous achievements were spread among several fields, but all originated in one central, spiritual motivation.

Schweitzer first chose to conduct his investigation of morality and divinity through scholarship. At the age of 18, he enrolled at the University of Strasbourg in Germany; six years later, he had earned a doctorate in philosophy. Additional study at the Sorbonne in France and the University of Berlin gained him an advanced degree in theology. At 27, he decided to accept an appointment to principal at St. Thomas College in Strasbourg, where his duties included lecturing in philosophy and theology. Before he was 30 years old, Schweitzer would publish several _____ (FIN) books on theology, including *The Quest of the Historical Jesus* and *The Mysticism of Paul the Apostle*.

At the same time that he was pursuing his degrees, Schweitzer was becoming an authority on the construction and music of the organ. His deep love for the instrument led him to a mastery of organ music and then to the publication of a book concerning the works of the composer Johann Sebastian Bach. In these endeavors, as in his studies, he did not neglect the spiritual aspect of his subject. His book primarily considers the religious nature of Bach's compositions.

Schweitzer's next career was in neither music nor theology, but still originated in his meditations on faith. After coming across a missionary publication containing an appeal for doctors in French Equatorial Africa, he decided to devote his life to practicing medicine in that region. Schweitzer's careful consideration of civilization and ethics convinced him that modern civilized society was stifling the dignity of non-white cultures and ethnicities and preventing such cultures from advancing. He wrote two books in which he explored the theory that the lack of progress in civilization was a result of an absence of "reverence for life." Having put forth some of his own ideas about the injustice he had discovered, he made plans to become a surgeon and to practice in the jungles of Africa.

When he was 38 years old, Albert Schweitzer carried out his plan. Armed with knowledge of and experience in medicine and surgery, he built a hospital in the French Congo. There, he and his wife, Helene, often operating under difficult conditions and in unsanitary environments, treated lepers and other patients. This work was to occupy Schweitzer for the rest of his life.

Albert Schweitzer's philosophy of compassion and respect for all humans, in addition to his many written works, won him the Nobel Peace Prize in 1952. It is clear, though, that recognition, whether for achievements in theological study, music, or medicine, meant far less to Schweitzer than did the opportunity to exercise and understand religious devotion and compassion. His _____ (NOV) ideas about the purpose of human life changed the way scholars and humanitarians thought about their mission in life. Many people are still following his example today.

1. According to the passage, which of the following statements about Schweitzer is true?
    A. He was a professor of music and a Lutheran minister.
    B. He was a man of many talents, as well as a humanitarian.
    C. He became a doctor after a missionary society rejected him.
    D. His musical talent kept him from being a doctor at an early age.

2. What is the main idea of the passage?
    A. Albert Schweitzer was interested in the theology of Johann Sebastian Bach.
    B. Albert Schweitzer was both a scholar and a humanitarian.
    C. Albert Schweitzer chose religion over medicine, then switched back.
    D. Albert Schweitzer lived according to his religious beliefs.

3. What is one way that the author proves the statement, "Even his many secular interests seemed to have been colored by religious yearning"?
    A. by describing Schweitzer's study of the religious aspects of Bach
    B. by noting the conditions under which Schweitzer operated
    C. by revealing that Schweitzer earned a degree in theology
    D. by noting Schweitzer's lack of concern about awards

Exercise VI. Drawing on your knowledge of roots and words in context, read the following selection and define the italicized words. If you cannot figure out the meaning of the words on your own, look them up in a dictionary. Note that the suffix *ordial* comes from the Latin *ordior*, which means "to begin." In addition, the prefix *re* means "again, back."

Many scientists consider the rain forests of South America and Southeast Asia the closest the modern world will ever get to true *primordial* landscapes. Unfortunately, as people continue to search for new sources of medicines, animal species, and wood, these rain forests are quickly being destroyed. Many fear that in a few years, trees from the rain forests, having been harvested for use in home *renovations*, will no longer shelter exotic birds and other animals. Environmentalists warn that this loss will affect us greatly.

UNIT THIRTEEN

ERR
Latin ERRARE, ERRATUM, "to wander"

ABERRANT   (a ber´ ənt)   *adj.*   deviating from a pattern or rule
L. *ab*, "away from" + *errare = wandering away from*
Since the data had previously been so consistent, the *aberrant* results puzzled the scientists.
syn: abnormal   *ant: typical*

ERRONEOUS   (e rō´ nē əs)   *adj.*   wrong or inaccurate
L. *erronis*, "straying from (the correct rule or standard)" from *errare*
Tina came to the understandable but *erroneous* conclusion that all dogs were unfriendly.
syn: mistaken   *ant: correct*

ERRANT   (er´ ənt)   *adj.*   wandering or straying
The *errant* knight soon found more adventure than he had bargained for.
syn: wayward

GRAD, GRESS
Latin GRADI, GRESSUM, "to go forth, to proceed"

DEGRADE   (dē grād´)   *v.*   to lower in dignity or esteem; to insult
L. *de*, "down" + *gradi = (to cause to) go down*
Hannah felt that the mayor's comment *degraded* women and should be withdrawn.
syn: belittle   *ant: honor*

CONGRESS   (kon´ gris)   *n.*   a coming together
L. *con*, "together" + *gressum = a proceeding together*
The meeting of scientists was hailed as "a *congress* of great minds."

EGRESS   (ē´ gres)   *n.*   the act of going out; an exit
L. *e*, "out of" + *gressum = going out*
The prisoners were taken to the *egress* after their court hearing.

VEN, VENT
Latin VENIRE, VENTUM, "to come"

CONVENE (kən vēn´) *v.* to call together; to assemble
L. *con*, "together" + *venire* = *to come together*
With the ringing of the bell, our chairman *convened* the fifth annual workshop.
syn: gather   *ant: adjourn*

COVENANT (kəv´ ən ənt) *n.* a mutual or legal agreement
Because the ancient *covenant* between the two tribes had been broken, a special meeting had to be called.
syn: contract

CIRCUMVENT (sûr kəm vent´) *v.* to avoid by going
   around; to bypass
L. *circum*, "around" + *ventum* = *to go around*
Harold attempted to *circumvent* the problem by planning ahead.
syn: sidestep   *ant: confront*

The traffic had to CIRCUMVENT the CIRCUS TENT that was set up in the middle of Main Street.

CUR, CURS
Latin CURRERE, CURSUM, "to run"

CURSORY (kûr´ sə rē) *adj.* hasty and superficial
Diane gave me a *cursory* wave as she was whisked away into the ballroom.
syn: casual   *ant: comprehensive*

PRECURSOR (prē kûr´ sər) *n.* that which comes before; a forerunner
L. *pre*, "before" + *currere* = *running before*
The shower of hail was only a *precursor* to the worst storm we had ever seen.
syn: harbinger

RECOURSE (rē´ kôrs) *n.* help for a problem; a solution
L. *re*, "back" + *currere* = *running back*
When Cameron needed help building the house, his only *recourse* was to go to his brother.
syn: resource

INCURSION (in kûr´ zhən) *n.* an attack on another's territory; an entering into
L. *in*, "into" + *currere* = *running into*
The soldier surveyed the damage after the enemy *incursion*.
syn: invasion

Ⅲ *Celebrities like using social media like Twitter and Facebook because it allows them to* circum-vent *reporters, studios, handlers, and executives so they can communicate directly with their fans.*

Ⅲ *How do you think a noun literally meaning "a running back" came to mean "a solution to a problem"?*

EXERCISES - UNIT THIRTEEN

Exercise I. Complete the sentence in a way that shows you understand the meaning of the italicized vocabulary word.

1.   The police officer feared that the minor crimes were *precursors* to larger ones because…

2.   Mary felt that the magazine article *degraded* scientists because it said…

3.   Although he did all he could to *circumvent* the city traffic, Mike…

4.   My last *recourse* when I couldn't get my car started was to…

5.   When Rose told Catherine about the tooth fairy, Catherine made the *erroneous* assumption that…

6.   We later learned that the *errant* golf ball that had struck a passerby was…

7.   Because I did only a *cursory* reading of the instructions on the test, I…

8.   A *congress* of local citizens gathered in the town square was able to…

9.   I panicked while in the amusement park's haunted house because the *egress*…

10.   When the king wanted to *convene* a council of wise men, he…

11.   Because none of the survey results on television we have gathered seems to be *aberrant*, we know that…

12.   If there is to be a *covenant* between the two nations, they must…

13.   After the small band of commandos made its first *incursion* into enemy territory…

Exercise II. Fill in the blank with the best word from the choices below. One word will not be used.

aberrant   errant   egress   cursory   circumvent

1.   If the _____ bullet had not hit a wall, someone could have been seriously injured.

2.   If we meet their demands, the kidnappers will allow the hostage _____.

3.   Even a(n) _____ glance at the room told the detective that something had gone horribly wrong.

4.   Is there any way to _____ the floods that come in the spring?

Fill in the blank with the best word from the choices below. One word will not be used.

covenant   congress   precursor   degrade   incursion

5.   A small _____ of local merchants had appeared on the village green.

6.   According to the _____ that is included in the contract, smoking is not allowed in the rental car at any time.

7.   The reviewer went so far as to personally _____ many actors, calling them "unfit to take the stage."

8.   The lawyer claimed, "This line of questioning by her ex-husband is an improper _____ into my client's personal religious beliefs and should not be allowed."

Fill in the blank with the best word from the choices below. One word will not be used.

cursory   erroneous   convene   recourse   precursor   aberrant

9.   When the medical tests showed that Ron was severely ill, he felt sure they were _____.

10.   Compared to the rest of the cells we have collected, this one, which is much bigger, seems _____.

11.   The judge _____ the court session by pounding her gavel.

12.   The horse and buggy was a(n) _____ to our modern automobile.

13.   Harriet felt she had no _____ but to go to the police with her information.

Exercise III. Choose the set of words that best completes the sentence.

1.   I don't mean to _____ our lecturer, but I think some of his conclusions were _____.
    A. convene; aberrant
    B. circumvent; errant
    C. convene; errant
    D. degrade; erroneous

2.   The first meeting that they _____ was only a(n) _____ to a much larger one held later that day.
    A. degraded; precursor
    B. convened; precursor
    C. degraded; covenant
    D. circumvented; egress

3.   When the sacred _____ between Lucile and her true love was broken, she felt she had no _____ except to find comfort in the Church.
     A.   covenant; recourse
     B.   congress; covenant
     C.   precursor; incursion
     D.   recourse; precursor

4.   The journalists visiting the war-torn country were refused _____ and decided to _____ the ruling by sneaking out of the country at night.
     A.   precursor; convene
     B.   covenant; degrade
     C.   egress; circumvent
     D.   incursion; degrade

5.   The soldier captured behind enemy lines denied he was on a(n) _____ into enemy territory; he said he was merely a(n) _____ traveler.
     A.   covenant; aberrant
     B.   incursion; errant
     C.   precursor; cursory
     D.   congress; cursory

Exercise IV. Complete the sentence by inferring information about the italicized word from its context.

1.   When Rob walks into a room where a camera has been secretly hidden and gives a *cursory* glance around the room, we can assume that…

2.   Immigrants who watch a television show that *degrades* people who legally come to America will likely…

3.   If a geologist testing the soil comes up with test results that seem to be *aberrant*, the geologist will probably…

Exercise V. Fill in each blank with the word from the Unit that best completes the sentence, using the root we supply as a clue. Then, answer the questions that follow the paragraphs.

In 1972, Congress, in an effort to end gender inequality in our nation's schools, approved the bill now known as Title IX. Leading to the passage of this law was the realization that young women did not have the academic, career, and sports opportunities afforded to their male peers. Title IX was controversial from the beginning, but nowhere did its implications meet with more resistance than in organized sports programs within the public schools.

High school sports have long been the domain of the male student population. It is boys' sports such as football that not only attract major crowds, but also serve as profitable enterprises for many large high school sports programs. Title IX has brought more money to women's sports, but it has not solved the gender gap.

Girls are still unable to find acceptance on traditionally male sports teams. In 1972, it was impossible for a female student to earn a spot on a high school football team. By 2016, there were still only a handful of young women who had earned the right to play football. Although girls' basketball is common, only rarely does a girl play basketball on the boys' team. Boys' basketball is more prestigious than girls' and remains more likely to attract attention and money to the school and individual players.

Young female athletes face sparse crowds and little support from school and parental organizations. While attendance at a boys' sports event may be standing room only, there are rarely sold-out crowds for even the best teams in girls' sports. The absence of fans to support winning teams in girls' sports is _____ (GRAD) to these young people.

In addition, because girls' sports have not yet gained the attention that traditional boys' sports have, there is less scholarship money available for women athletes. Seventy-two percent of high school athletic scholarships are still awarded to boys. Young women with athletic talents occasionally do win these awards, but usually end up earning less money and prestige.

Although Title IX has made opportunities more accessible to young women, thirty years after its passage, its sports benefits are still relatively insignificant. Many believe, _____ (ERR), that Title IX brought gender equity to sports programs and individuals in our public schools. Until society accepts the value of girls in sports, young women will not have earned the equality promised by Title IX.

1.   According to the author, Title IX's success rate has been
    A. outstanding.
    B. good.
    C. fair.
    D. poor.

2.   Which sentence best describes the main idea of this piece?
    A. In 1972, Congress passed Title IX in an effort to end gender inequality in our nation's schools.
    B. High school sports have long been the domain of the male student population.
    C. Thirty years after Title IX's passage, its benefits are still relatively insignificant.
    D. Girls are still unable to find acceptance on traditionally boys' sports teams.

3.   Which of the following statements is NOT true, according to the passage?
    A. Title IX is controversial thirty years after its passage.
    B. Boys' sports are more important than girls' sports.
    C. Twenty-eight percent of athletic scholarships are awarded to girls.
    D. Girls can and do play on some boys' sports teams.

Exercise VI. Drawing on your knowledge of roots and words in context, read the following selection and define the italicized words. If you cannot figure out the meaning of the words on your own, look them up in a dictionary. Note that the prefix *re* means "back" and *trans* means "beyond."

During the latest three-day outdoor music festival known as Woodstock, many people at the concert *regressed* to primitive behavior. The crowd of young adults and teenagers acted more like untamed beasts than civilized human beings. Their uncontrolled behavior, ranging from rioting to rolling in the mud, *transgressed* the rules of social acceptability. Following the festival, there was a movement toward more crowd control and tighter security at concerts.

UNIT FOURTEEN

VIR

Latin VIR, "man"

When Eric looked in the mirror, he
saw a VIRILE VIKING.

VIRILE (vēr´ əl) *adj.* masculine; manly
Will tried to prove he was strong and *virile* by lifting the
enormous refrigerator.

ant: weak

VIRTUE (vûr´ chōō) *n.* the right action; moral goodness
It takes a special kind of *virtue* to do good acts and never seek recognition for
them.

ant: vice

VIRTUOSO (vûr chōō ō´ sō) *n.* someone extraordinarily skilled in a particular art
Frank was a piano *virtuoso*; he could play very difficult pieces by ear.

DEM

Greek DEMOS, "people"

DEMAGOGUE (dem´ ə gäg) *n.* a leader who appeals to people's emotions to
   gain power
G. *demos* + *agein*, "to lead" = *one who leads people*
Some voters feared our governor, whose opinions seemed to change depending
on his audience, was in danger of becoming a *demagogue*.

DEMOGRAPHIC (dem ə graf´ ik) *adj.* having certain characteristics in
   common such as age, race, or gender
G. *demos* + *graphy*, "study of" = *the study of people*
The company targeted a very specific *demographic* group with a new series of
advertisements aimed at teenagers.

PANDEMIC (pan dem´ ik) *adj.* having an effect on a large area or region
G. *pan*, "all" + *demos* = *all people*
The mysterious disease seemed to be *pandemic* among the inhabitants of the
country.
syn: rampant   *ant: confined*

To the Romans, a vir was
a man, and virtus, which
came into English as
virtue, was all that was
best about a man's
physical and moral being:
courage, strength, skill,
and nobility. Today, of
course, both men and
women can be virtuous.

Democracy, literally
meaning "power of the
people," is what allows
us all to have a say in
our government. But a
demagogue, a "people
leader," takes advantage
of the people to gain
power for himself or
herself.

In order to successfully
sell a product, a marketing
professional must think of
the demographic group
that will receive the
advertisement. If a
commercial on television,
for instance, is shown to
senior citizens, but is
designed for a
demographic group that
includes children, the
product will probably not
sell very well.

POLIT
Greek POLIS, "city"

COSMOPOLITAN (käz mə päl´ i tən) *adj.* worldly or sophisticated
G. *cosmos*, "world" + *polis* = *being a citizen of the world*
While Wendy's husband thought the restaurant had an appealing *cosmopolitan*
flavor, her mother thought the whole place rather snobbish.
syn: cultured   *ant: unpolished*

POLITICIZE (pə lit´ i sīz) *v.* to give a political character to something
Some people criticize the president for *politicizing* the shootings.

APOLITICAL (ā pə lit´ i kəl) *adj.* having no interest in politics; not political
G. *a*, "not" + *politikos* (from *polis*) = *not political*
Many people who were once *apolitical* turned out to vote in the recent elections.

CIVIS
Latin CIVIS, "citizen"

CIVILITY (si vil´ i tē) *n.* politeness; courteousness
Although my brother and I fought constantly, we treated each other with *civility* in
public.
syn: decorum   *ant: rudeness*

CIVIC (siv´ ik) *adj.* having to do with the business of a town or community
Mrs. Morita considers it her *civic* duty to attend the town meetings.

CIVILIZE (siv´ ə līz) *v.* to make more cultured or refined
My mother's attempt to *civilize* her wild children only made us more determined
to do whatever we wanted.
syn: polish

▣ In ancient Greece, the
polis, *or city-state, was
the center of
government, art, and
culture (Athens and
Sparta are the two most
famous examples). Just
as a voting member of
one of our modern cities
is a citizen, a voting
member of the* polis *was
called a* politikos. *We
get our word* political
from politikos.

▣ *The civility which
money will purchase, is
rarely extended to those
who have none.*
—Charles Dickens

EXERCISES – UNIT FOURTEEN

Exercise I. Complete the sentence in a way that shows you understand the meaning of the italicized vocabulary word.

1.   To express their *civic* pride, the Johnson family…

2.   With her stylish car and *cosmopolitan* wardrobe, Bette looked like someone who…

3.   Many fans considered Jimmy a tennis *virtuoso* because he…

4.   The *demographic* group targeted by the ice cream company was…

5.   A small group of citizens tried to *politicize* the town meeting by…

6.   We could tell the young wrestler was *virile* because he…

7.   The most important *virtue* to have as a firefighter is probably…

8.   The pioneers tried to *civilize* the frontier by…

9.   Although the charity organization claimed to be *apolitical*,…

10. Because Margaret exercised *civility* towards Troy after he had hurt her feelings, Troy…

11. A rabble-rouser and a *demagogue*, the candidate traveled around the state, looking to…

12. Once the doctors were certain that polio was *pandemic* in the city's population, they…

Exercise II. Fill in the blank with the best word from the choices below. One word will not be used.

politicize   virtue   virtuoso   pandemic   civilize

1.   It would be unfortunate if money were able to _____ a group that has worked so hard to avoid endorsing a candidate.

2.   If I cannot _____ my rowdy dogs within a few weeks, my neighbors are going to start complaining.

3.   Patience was a _____ that my grandmother had in abundance.

4.   The Buddhist speaker said that greed is _____ in the Western world.

Fill in the blank with the best word from the choices below. One word will not be used.

civic	virile	demagogue	apolitical	demographic

5. Do you think the president is charming and charismatic, or is he a(n) _____ who might eventually abuse the power he gains?

6. To what _____ portion of the state is this political campaign appealing?

7. To prove that he is _____, a male gorilla will beat his chest and tear leaves from the trees.

8. Oliver, who once considered himself _____, is now campaigning for the governor.

Fill in the blank with the best word from the choices below. One word will not be used.

virtuoso	civilize	civic	civility	cosmopolitan

9. To Libby, taking a limousine uptown felt very glamorous and _____.

10. Roger felt it was his _____ responsibility to pick up litter and sweep the sidewalk in the town.

11. Rather than trying to prove she was a ballet _____, Amelia decided to show the audition judges the passion she felt for her art.

12. If Liam and Jane could show _____ to one another for even a minute, there would be no more fighting in the house.

Exercise III. Choose the set of words that best completes the sentence.

1. One _____ of being as _____ as my uncle is having the ability to share interesting information about the world.
    A. demagogue; apolitical
    B. virtue; cosmopolitan
    C. virtuoso; civic
    D. civility; virile

2. When Annette refused to criticize any of the local candidates, was she being _____ or just _____ and polite?
    A. cosmopolitan; civic
    B. demographic; virile
    C. virile; pandemic
    D. apolitical; civil

3. Although the general said he was not using force, only strict laws to _____ the country, some people feared he was a _____ who would abuse his power.
    A. civilize; virtuoso
    B. politicize; virtue
    C. civilize; demagogue
    D. politicize; virtuoso

4. We knew that repression had become _____ when a shy little flute _____ was arrested for anti-government activities.
    A. pandemic; virtuoso
    B. demographic; virtue
    C. virile; demagogue
    D. politic; virtuoso

5. A group of _____-minded local citizens published a report on the _____ make up of the town.
    A. virile; apolitical
    B. cosmopolitan; civic
    C. civic; demographic
    D. demographic; pandemic

Exercise IV. Complete the sentence by inferring information about the italicized word from its context.

1. If someone driving by a billboard sees that it features a tractor, a cornfield, and a barn, he or she might guess that the *demographic*…

2. Listening to a recording of a guitarist, Joe exclaimed, "What a *virtuoso*!" We can assume the guitarist is…

3. When a teacher in a kindergarten class wants her students to use *civility* toward one another, she will probably encourage them to…

Exercise V. Fill in each blank with the word from the Unit that best completes the sentence, using the root we supply as a clue. Then, answer the questions that follow the paragraphs.

Among the first European settlers in America were the Puritans, who, fleeing religious persecution in Europe, settled the Massachusetts Bay Colony in 1630. John Winthrop, their leader, was a religious man who later became the governor of the Massachusetts Bay Colony. As the colonists were making their way across the Atlantic Ocean, Winthrop delivered a sermon to them containing his vision of what the new country was to be like. It would be a place, he said, where people would be allowed to worship as they chose, but the government would be partially controlled by the Church. John Winthrop and the Puritans did not imagine any separation between religious and _____ (CIVIS) institutions in the new America. The country had to go through many changes before the doctrine of the separation of Church and State, which we take for granted today, was adopted.

What happened to alter the Puritans' concept of government? Much of the shift can be attributed to the thinking, writings, and persuasive actions of Thomas Jefferson, that well-traveled, well-read, _____ (POLIT) man of the late 1700s and early 1800s. Jefferson's desire to incorporate the ideal of religious freedom into the laws of the United

States accounts almost fully for our country's early switch to a non-sectarian government. He had a vision of a nation whose affairs would, under the Constitution, be totally separate from the institutions of religion.

In 1777, Jefferson, who sat in the General Assembly of the State of Virginia, wrote a bill calling for the establishment of religious freedom in Virginia. Because of the varying opinions held by lawmakers at that time, we can only imagine that the debate before passage must have been heated. However, the bill was adopted in the Virginia Assembly on January 16, 1786, and subsequently served as a model for the First Amendment of the Constitution.

Freedom of religion is now guaranteed to all Americans under this amendment, which states, "Congress shall make no law respecting an establishment of religion or prohibiting the free exercise thereof." The guarantee, however, has proven to be a controversial one throughout US history. In the 1800s, for instance, the government prohibited certain Mormon beliefs because such beliefs were in conflict with United States laws. During the same period, some Native American tribes were also denied their religious practices.

Since that time, the separation of Church and State in America has evolved and changed. Americans have seen the legality of individual religious freedoms continue to be tested and the Constitution of the United States reinterpreted in numerous ways. Even today, though, the disputes go on: public displays of religious material and the legality of prayer in school settings stir up strong feelings in every community. It appears that "freedom of religion," like religion itself, will never mean the same thing to everyone.

1. John Winthrop seemed to envision the Puritan settlement in America as
    A. a commune in which everyone could do as he or she pleased.
    B. a settlement in which various religions could live together peacefully, but with separate community governments.
    C. a place in which religious and civic authorities would share power.
    D. a temporary shelter from the religious persecutions of Europe.

2. The man who finally accomplished the passage of the Virginia Act for Establishing Religious Freedom in Virginia in 1786 was
    A. Thomas Jefferson.
    B. John Winthrop.
    C. an unknown Puritan.
    D. an unknown Mormon Elder.

3. Which statement is correct about the information in the passage?
    A. The author is in favor of religious practice being mandated by the State.
    B. The author would be against setting up a Nativity scene at City Hall.
    C. The author supports Jefferson's idea of Church and State separation.
    D. The author expresses no opinion about the separation of Church and State.

Exercise VI. Drawing on your knowledge of roots and words in context, read the following selection and define the italicized words. If you cannot figure out the meaning of the words on your own, look them up in a dictionary. Note that the prefix *tri* means "three" and that the prefix *mega* means "great, large."

Pompey, Caesar, Crassus. Antony, Lepidus, Octavian. Six of the Roman Empire's greatest generals and politicians joined forces to create two *triumvirates*. The first *triumvirate* was formed by Gnaeus Pompey, Julius Caesar, and Marcus Crassus. The three joined in 60 BCE to share control of the Roman Empire. The second *triumvirate* was formed by Marc Antony, Marcus Lepidus, and Octavian. Both groupings lead to the eventual control by a single ruler, as two of the men in each trio were killed in military battles. Under the rule of both *triumvirates*, the boundaries of the Empire were extended throughout Europe, Asia, and Africa; Rome, with its diverse population and unprecedented size, had become a true *megalopolis*.

UNIT FIFTEEN

DIC, DICT
Latin DICERE, DICTUM, "to say; to order"

DICTATE   (dik´ tāt)   v.   1. to speak aloud in order that one's words may be copied or recorded
2. to give an order; to make necessary
1. Regina *dictated* a letter for her secretary.
2. Our current circumstances *dictate* that we conserve money and resources.
syn: demand

MALEDICTION   (mal ə dik´ shən)   n.   a recital of words intended to harm; a curse
L. *male*, "badly" + *dicere = speaking badly (of one)*
To Claudia, Leo's angry words were practically a *malediction*.

BENEDICTION   (ben ə dik´ shən)   n.   a blessing
L. *bene*, "well" + *dictum = to speak well*
A local rabbi started the ceremony by giving a *benediction* to the audience.

LOC, LOQU
Latin LOQUI, LOCUTUS, "to speak"

LOCUTION   (lō kyōō´ shən)   n.   a style or action of speaking
Nothing about Francis's careful *locution* betrayed his nervousness.

ELOQUENT   (el´ ə kwənt)   adj.   powerful and expressive
Brenda composed an *eloquent* tribute for her younger sister's wedding.
syn: articulate   *ant: ineffective*

COLLOQUIAL   (kə lō´ kwē əl)   adj.   of or related to informal speech; conversational
L. *con*, "together" + *loqui = to speak together*
When the residents of Stoneville were interviewed on television, they dropped some of their *colloquial* expressions in favor of more formal language.
syn: idiomatic

Another name for "word choice" is diction. An author's diction can convey the tone of a work.

Ventriloquism, literally meaning "wind-speech," is the art of "throwing your voice."

VOCA

Latin VOCARE, VOCATUM, "to call"

EVOCATIVE (ē väk´ ə tiv) *adj.* calling forth a vivid image or impression
L. *e*, "out of" + *vocatum* = *to call out (of memory or mind)*
The novel features an *evocative* description of a lakeside town in Michigan.
syn: suggestive

EQUIVOCATE (ē kwiv´ ə kāt) *v.* to use misleading or confusing language
L. *equi*, "equal" + *vocare* = *to say (two things) equally*
Because Shonda felt it her duty never to *equivocate* to a client, she made a point of
discussing all sides of every problem.
syn: evade

ADVOCATE (ad´ və kāt) *v.* 1. to argue in favor of
             (ad´ və kət) *n.* 2. someone who argues for
L. *ad*, "toward" + *vocare* = *to call to toward*
1. The senator plans to *advocate* capital punishment for those convicted of murder.
syn: recommend   *ant: oppose*
2. As an *advocate* of careful financial planning, I cannot go along with your plan
   to invest in a bubble-gum factory.
syn: supporter   *ant: enemy*

> ▥ *Your vocation is your job or profession; your avocation is a hobby or a leisure activity.*

CLAM, CLAIM

Latin CLAMARE, CLAMATUM, "to shout or call"

EXCLAMATORY (eks klam´ ə tôr ē) *adj.* having a forceful, excited, or
    emotional tone
L. *ex*, "out of" + *clamare* = *shouting out*
Mr. Litt is famous for the *exclamatory* style of his speeches.

DECLAIM (dē klām´) *v.* to speak loudly and with feeling
L. *de*, "down from" + *clamare* = *to shout down from*
Martin *declaimed* upon the subject of tax hikes until the audience was completely
bored.

CLAMOROUS (klam´ ər əs) *adj.* characterized by a
    loud noise or outcry
The pianist entered the auditorium to *clamorous* applause.
syn: ear-splitting   *ant: quiet*

> ▥ *To declaim can mean either "to make a formal speech," as in the sentence "Young George will declaim upon the topic in the rhetorical exhibition," or "to rant," as in the sentence at left.*

The crowd was so CLAMOROUS that the
GLAMOROUS singer could not be heard.

EXERCISES - UNIT FIFTEEN

Exercise I. Complete the sentence in a way that shows you understand the meaning of the italicized vocabulary word.

1.   The *eloquent* tribute by Lorenzo to his former teacher made her feel...

2.   During the *benediction*, the speaker told the graduating class that...

3.   As an *advocate* of weaker environmental laws, Janet believes...

4.   When asked whether he had witnessed the crime, the man *equivocated*, saying...

5.   Nicole spoke *colloquial* English only when she was...

6.   Philip's financial difficulties *dictate* that he...

7.   The *evocative* lyrics about the canals of old Venice made me...

8.   The young debater's flawless *locution* made him seem...

9.   The movie's hero utters a *malediction* against his enemy when...

10.   The *clamorous* shrieking of the monkeys high above caused the explorers to...

11.   Preacher Bell's *exclamatory* sermons often prompted members of the congregation to...

12.   Anton angrily *declaimed* about the score he had received, but the judges...

Exercise II. Fill in the blank with the best word from the choices below. One word will not be used.

colloquial   locution   evocative   dictate   malediction

1.   If you have ever learned a foreign language, you know that _____ speech is very different from formal speech.

2.   The hockey league let the temperature inside the arena _____ the game schedule.

3.   While I think the writer has some talent, his language is not _____ of the places he describes.

4.   Having uttered a powerful _____ against his evil uncle, the prince departed the kingdom.

Fill in the blank with the best word from the choices below. One word will not be used.

locution   equivocate   eloquent   advocate   benediction

5. Carla gave a(n) _____ speech in honor of the bride, and everyone applauded.

6. Miss Hutchins, the second-grade teacher, never allowed her students to _____; she wanted a "yes" or "no" answer.

7. Tommy's _____ reveals that he is a trained Shakespearean actor.

8. While composing the _____ for the ceremony, the leader thought carefully about what he wanted to say.

Fill in the blank with the best word from the choices below. One word will not be used.

equivocate   declaim   clamorous   advocate   exclamatory

9. I am a(n) _____ of child safety, but I also think children should be given some freedom.

10. Lisa heard the _____ wailing of the babies long before she reached the nursery.

11. On what dull topic must we listen to the professor _____ today?

12. The radio host's remarks always struck me as overly energetic and _____.

Exercise III. Choose the set of words that best completes the sentence.

1. Although Graham is a both an excellent scholar and a(n) _____ speaker, he always tries to _____ any praise he receives.
   A. evocative; equivocate
   B. eloquent; deflect
   C. colloquial; dictate
   D. evocative; declaim

2. Because I believe that the population increase _____ that we build more houses, I am a(n) _____ of development in this area.
   A. declaims; malediction
   B. dictates; advocate
   C. equivocates; locution
   D. declaims; advocate

3. The poet _____ endlessly upon the harm that technology has done to the world, but I find his words and images beautifully _____ of the places he describes.
    A. equivocates; clamorous
    B. advocates; exclamatory
    C. advocates; colloquial
    D. declaims; evocative

4. In a rather _____ letter expressing his outrage, Martin did not _____ about who was to blame for the crime in the city.
    A. exclamatory; advocate
    B. exclamatory; equivocate
    C. eloquent; dictate
    D. colloquial; advocate

5. When the singer visiting the small town smiled and uttered a(n) _____ phrase common only in that region, the audience burst into _____ cheers.
    A. exclamatory; evocative
    B. eloquent; colloquial
    C. colloquial; clamorous
    D. evocative; eloquent

Exercise IV. Complete the sentence by inferring information about the italicized word from its context.

1. If Cynthia directs a *malediction* at Jake, we can assume that she…

2. If you *advocate* being constantly prepared, and you see me with an umbrella, you will probably tell me…

3. When writing an evaluation of the actor's *locution*, the acting coach will probably consider things like…

Exercise V. Fill in each blank with the word from the Unit that best completes the sentence, using the root we supply as a clue. Then, answer the questions that follow the paragraphs.

According to the Environmental Protection Agency, Earth's surface temperature has risen one degree Fahrenheit over the past century. This gradual process is called climate change, and although one degree in a hundred years does not seem like much to most people, many scientists and environmentalists warn that it can be devastating to the earth's environment. For this reason, they _____ (VOCA) major reforms in the practices that led to this problem. Man, they say, would be naïve to believe that his activities have no impact on the environment.

A changing climate is not, by nature, a bad thing. In fact, it is a necessity for life on Earth. The sun's energy sets Earth's climate in motion; Earth, in turn, radiates energy back into space. Greenhouse gases such as methane and carbon dioxide trap some of that energy, helping to keep the earth warm. If this natural process, called the greenhouse effect, did not occur, the earth would become too cold to sustain life. In recent years, however, the greenhouse effect has been unusually strong, causing dramatic shifts in climate and weather worldwide. What could explain this sudden change in a previously balanced system?

A growing body of scientists now believes that since the Industrial Revolution of the nineteenth century, human activities have significantly contributed to the rise in temperature of the atmosphere. The International Panel on Climate Control (IPCC) has stated that human beings have a discernible influence on Earth's climate and that the warming trend is probably not entirely natural in origin. The Panel points out that increased use of motor vehicles, heating and cooling of houses, operation of factories, and harvesting of timber all add to the gases that alter the chemical composition of the earth's atmosphere.

Scientists have reason to be concerned. As warmer temperatures cause ice and snow in the Poles to melt, global sea levels begin to rise. In addition, atmospheric changes are increasing the annual amount of rainfall worldwide. The combined overabundance of water can result in the submersion of coastal lands once used to support food crops or residential areas. And the loss of these lands is not the only disturbing pattern. Disruptive climatic changes can lead to the extinction of various forms of life on Earth, and the composition of the air human beings breathe is being affected in ways that may contribute to the ill health of millions.

If human beings are indeed responsible for global climate alteration, they must take measures to reverse the damage to the planet. The replacement of gas-burning motor vehicles by electric ones would be a step in the right direction, as would stricter preservation of the world's rain forests. But these small steps may ultimately not be sufficient, given the rapid growth of industry and population. For this reason, many environmentalists believe that the precarious ecological situation _____ (DIC) that humankind change many of its attitudes and practices, regardless of politics and economics.

1.   The author of the passage would probably disagree with which of the following statements?
     A. People are the primary cause of the world's changing climate.
     B. Small steps like electric cars are not enough to stop climate change.
     C. Rising sea levels will probably force a change in humans' way of life.
     D. The climate will heal itself without humans changing their behavior.

2.   What is the purpose of the third paragraph?
     A. to explain how global warming is a harmful natural phenomenon
     B. to show that global warming is made harmful by human beings
     C. to argue that global warming is a social and economic dilemma
     D. to reevaluate the validity of the claims of environmentalists

3.   Which of the following is NOT mentioned as being a result of climate change?
     A. stronger storms
     B. species extinction
     C. melting of polar ice
     D. warmer temperatures

Exercise VI. Drawing on your knowledge of roots and words in context, read the following selection and define the italicized words. If you cannot figure out the meaning of the words on your own, look them up in a dictionary. Note that the prefix *ab* means "away from," *re* means "back," and *ir* is a form of *in*, meaning "not."

On December 10, 1936, King Edward VIII of England became the first, and only, British monarch to voluntarily *abdicate* the throne. Edward gave up his crown after falling in love with a married woman, Wallis Warfield Simpson. Edward unsuccessfully attempted to win over the rest of the royal family in support of his love. When he realized the cause was lost, Edward gave up his claim to the throne, proclaiming, "I, Edward,...do hereby declare my *irrevocable* determination to renounce the throne for myself and my descendants." After his retirement, he accepted the title of Governor of the Bahamas.

UNIT SIXTEEN

CRUX
Latin CRUX, "cross"

EXCRUCIATING (eks krōō´ shē āt ing) *adj.* extremely painful; agonizing
L. *ex*, "out of" + *crux* = *from the cross*
Min was forced to sit through an *excruciating* series of piano recitals.
syn: unbearable　　　　　　　　*ant: pleasant*

CRUX (kruks) *n.* the most important or decisive point
The *crux* of the matter is the difference between children and adults.
syn: essence　　　　　　　　*ant: extra*

CRUCIAL (krōō´shəl) *adj.* necessary; essential
Good study skills are often *crucial* to success in high school and college.
　　　　　　　　ant: unimportant

DOL
Latin DOLERE, "to feel pain; to be grieved"

INDOLENT (in´ də lənt) *adj.* lazy; averse to work
L. *in*, "not" + *dolere* = *feeling no pain*
Being of a somewhat *indolent* character, Paige was not inclined to take on extra jobs.
syn: listless　　　　　　　*ant: robust*

DOLEFUL (dōl´ fəl) *adj.* sad; mournful
You can tell by Greg's constantly *doleful* expression that he has a gloomy nature.
syn: depressed　　　　　　*ant: cheerful*

DOLOROUS (dōl´ ər əs) *adj.* mournful; gloomy
The *dolorous* chanting of the monks was made even sadder by the steady, gray rain.
syn: bleak　　　　　　　*ant: uplifting*

▥ Crucifixion, *or "execution by cross," was fairly common in ancient Rome. Thus the word* crux, *"cross," became associated with torture. Later,* crux *came to mean "a crossroads, a decision point"—something that determines what is most important. From this second meaning, we get our words* crux *and* crucial.

▥ *How do you think we got a word meaning "lazy" from a root that means "to feel no pain"?*

ACRI, ACER
Latin ACER, "sharp"

ACERBIC (ə sûr´ bik) *adj.* harsh and biting in tone
L. *acerbus*, "sharp, biting" (from *acer*)
Cal's *acerbic* reply to the reporters earned him a reputation as an ill-tempered man.
syn: *sharp*   ant: *bland*

ACRID (ak´ rid) *adj.* stinging or biting in odor or
     taste; harsh; irritating
The *acrid* fumes that filled the office soon had us coughing and rubbing our eyes.

ACK!!! RID us of that ACRID odor!!

ACRIMONIOUS (ak rə mō´ nē əs) *adj.* exhibiting
     harsh sharpness in speech or mood
L. *acer*, "sharp" + *mony*, "quality of" = *having a sharp, bitter quality*
The *acrimonious* debate between the two candidates did not help either one in the polls.
syn: *bitter*   ant: *civil*

EXACERBATE (eg za´ sər bāt) *v.* to make worse or more severe
L. *ex*, "out of" + *acer* = *to make (something) harsher out of*
Mira's comments, which were supposed to be helpful, only *exacerbated* Shelley's problem.
syn: *aggravate*   ant: *ease*

> ▥ *Speaking* acrimoniously *or attacking someone personally in an argument does nothing more than* exacerbate *the argument.*

FERV
Latin FERVERE, "to boil; to be warm"

FERVENT (fûr´ vənt) *adj.* passionately excited or enthusiastic
Grace, a *fervent* supporter of the N.R.A, cheered enthusiastically when her favorite candidate was nominated.
syn: *fiery*   ant: *indifferent*

FERVOR (fûr´ vər) *n.* emotional excitement; heated enthusiasm
The *fervor* Ron displays when discussing cars lets me know he'll make a great mechanic.
syn: *eagerness*   ant: *apathy*

EFFERVESCENT (e fər ves´ ənt) *adj.* highly spirited; animated
L. *ex*, "out of" + *fervere* = *boiling out of*
The young horse had a cheerful, almost *effervescent* character.
syn: *bubbly*   ant: *lifeless*

> ▥ *Why do you think someone in high spirits would be called* effervescent?

EXERCISES - UNIT SIXTEEN

Exercise I. Complete the sentence in a way that shows you understand the meaning of the italicized vocabulary word.

1.   The *effervescent* cheering of the fans in the stands caused the team to…

2.   The *doleful* mood that Luke has been in recently is a result of…

3.   When the *acrid* city air blew into our faces, we…

4.   The mayor wanted to get to the *crux* of the matter because…

5.   On one particularly *excruciating* exam day, I felt…

6.   The *indolent* nature of the two sisters was apparent when they…

7.   We could tell the argument had become *acrimonious* when…

8.   Trisha's desire to see the band was obviously *fervent* because…

9.   When Mission Control told the astronaut that fixing the part was *crucial*, he…

10.   If you find that the medicine *exacerbates* your problem, you should…

11.   When Cynthia heard the *dolorous* song, she felt…

12.   Lulu was *acerbic* when she spoke to Adam because…

Exercise II. Fill in the blank with the best word from the choices below. One word will not be used.

indolent   dolorous   crux   fervent   excruciating

1.   The _____ of the problem is that my friend and I fight constantly.

2.   Because you are _____, you just want to sit around and eat potato chips, but you should get some exercise instead.

3.   It is George's _____ hope that his favorite actress will answer his letters.

4.   The critic wrote, "The film is so awful that just sitting through it caused me _____ pain."

Fill in the blank with the best word from the choices below. One word will not be used.

doleful	acrid	acerbic	exacerbate	acrimonious

5.   The gloomy colors of the room seemed to _____ the sadness that Joyce felt.

6.   The twins had a really _____ fight, and they hurt each other's feelings deeply.

7.   When Francoise heard the _____ whistle of a lonely train, she began to weep.

8.   If you are less _____ to the children when they ask questions, they won't think of you as grumpy.

Fill in the blank with the best word from the choices below. One word will not be used.

crux	fervor	acrid	crucial	effervescent

9.   Hilda was amazed at the _____ Tim displayed when talking about his beloved model trains.

10.   It is _____ that we reach the trapped skiers before the temperature drops.

11.   If the fumes of the factory are so _____ that your eyes burn, you should stay out of that area.

12.   I felt such _____ happiness that I seemed to be floating instead of walking.

Exercise III. Choose the set of words that best completes the sentence.

1.   In his typical sarcastic, _____ way, Robin sneered that I was too _____ to accomplish any work at all.
    A.   effervescent; acrid
    B.   acerbic; indolent
    C.   doleful; acerbic
    D.   excruciating; crucial

2.   Michael knew it was _____ for him to pull himself out of his _____ mood, so he tried to think of happy things.
    A.   acrid; fervent
    B.   indolent; acrimonious
    C.   excruciating; effervescent
    D.   crucial; dolorous

3.   I am afraid that Clark's wish to own a motorcycle is so _____ that seeing any vehicle—car, bicycle, or otherwise—will only _____ the problem.
      A. fervent; exacerbate
      B. acerbic; exacerbate
      C. effervescent; exacerbate
      D. acrid; exacerbate

4.   Sherry switched rapidly from the bitterness of the _____ screaming match to the _____ cheerfulness she needed for the party.
      A. acrimonious; effervescent
      B. dolorous; excruciating
      C. fervent; acrid
      D. acrid; doleful

5.   The _____ of our city's problem is the _____, polluted air caused by factories and cars, as well as by residents burning trash.
      A. fervor; acrid
      B. fervor; fervent
      C. crux; acrid
      D. crux; effervescent

Exercise IV. Complete the sentence by inferring information about the italicized word from its context.

1.   If Laurie displays a *fervor* for her religion, Pete can assume her experiences in her church have been…

2.   The children seem rather *indolent* to their grandmother; she might suspect the children's parents have not…

3.   If Jill's attempt to settle an argument between Steve and Dave *exacerbates* the situation, she will probably…

Exercise V. Fill in each blank with the word from the Unit that best completes the sentence, using the root we supply as a clue. Then, answer the questions that follow the paragraphs.

In addition to being the coldest place on Earth, Antarctica is the world's largest desert. With an average of two inches of precipitation per year in its central regions, Antarctica remains covered by ice only because the little snowfall each year doesn't thaw. Due to these barren conditions, Antarctica has never supported human beings or large land animals. The birds and seals that spend their time on Antarctica's coasts depend on the surrounding waters for sustenance. Encompassing Antarctica are seas rich in plankton (microscopic marine algae), which serve as food for tiny, shrimp-like krill. Krill, in turn, are a(n) _____ (CRUX) food source for the whales, seals, and penguins of Antarctica.

The abundance of fur seals, elephant seals, and various types of whales has brought international attention to Antarctica. Between 1784 and 1822, Europeans hunted millions of fur seals for their skins along Antarctic coasts. The skins were prepared for trade with China, which was an extremely profitable venture at the time. Whale hunters, who sold whale oil for use as lamp fuel, sailed south during this period, but were unable to capture the fast-moving Antarctic rorquals. Instead, they hunted elephant seals and rendered them into oil as a substitution for whale oil. At times, when the elephant seals became scarce, hunters also targeted penguins for their oil. The penguin population, however, was not devastated to the same degree as the seal colonies were. Commercial interests in seals during this era left the fur and elephant seal populations near extinction. By the end of the nineteenth century, the seal population was recovering, but the presence of hunters searching for whales near Antarctica again resulted in the slaughter of elephant seals for their oil.

Advancements in whaling technology brought whalers back to the shores of Antarctica in 1904. Faster catch boats and explosive harpoons allowed whalers to finally capture the humpback and blue whales they sought in the South, as well as exhaust the supply of whales in northern waters. England and Norway dominated the industry initially, but Japanese hunters took the lead in the 1930s. By 1965, hunters had killed hundreds of thousands of whales off the shores of Antarctica, and the whale population was less than 10% of its original size. The International Whaling Commission imposed a moratorium on commercial whaling in 1968, in an attempt to salvage the whale population. The restriction remains in place today.

Although seals of all types have increased in number since the last surge of hunting in the 1890s, the population of Antarctic whales has not significantly improved, despite nearly 50 years of their being protected. The effects of this decreased number of whales on that continent's ecosystem are currently under scientific investigation.

1. What would be an appropriate title for this passage?
   A. Antarctica's Imbalanced Ecosystem
   B. The Exploration of Antarctica
   C. Hunting Antarctica's Seals and Whales
   D. The World's Vastest Desert

2. From its use in the passage, what do you think a "rorqual" is?
   A. a whale
   B. a seal
   C. a penguin
   D. a boat

3. What is krill, and why is it important in the Antarctic waters?
   A. Krill is a marine algae and is important because sea creatures depend on it.
   B. Krill is a type of whale that has been a main target for hunters in Antarctica.
   C. Krill is a crustacean that marine algae depend on for food.
   D. Krill is a shrimp-like food source for large animals in the Antarctic waters.

Exercise VI. Drawing on your knowledge of roots and words in context, read the following selection and define the italicized words. If you cannot figure out the meaning of the words on your own, look them up in a dictionary. Note that the prefix *con* means "with."

Mrs. Hanson had always been a *fervid* supporter of the Republican Party. In addition to working long hours putting up flyers and attending rallies during the week, she spent many Saturdays doing extra work for her local chapter. When she was forced to give up her job campaigning for the Party to take care of her ailing husband, her fellow campaigners missed her very much. When Mrs. Hanson's husband died, many local politicians came to express their *condolences* to their bereaved coworker.

UNIT SEVENTEEN

PUT
Latin PUTARE, PUTATUM, "to think"

IMPUTE   (im pūt´)   *v.*   to assign blame or responsibility for
L. *in*, "on, against" + *putare* = *to think against*
The car's manufacturer *imputed* the steering problems to faulty tires.
syn: attribute   *ant: vindicate*

DISPUTE   (dis pūt´)   *v.*   1. to disagree with
                             n.   2. a disagreement or argument
L. *dis*, "apart" + *putare* = *to think apart*
1. Lisa *disputed* my claim that she was always late; in
fact, she said, she was usually early.
syn: deny   *ant: agree*
2. The city council was divided by the *dispute* over sales
taxes.
syn: argument   *ant: agreement*

CLUTE'S DISPUTE over falling leaves was solved with a chainsaw.

DISREPUTABLE   (dis rep´ yōō tə bəl)   *adj.*   not respectable;
having a bad reputation
L. *dis*, "bad" + *re*, "again" + *putare* = *thought badly of again
and again*
The *disreputable* doctor allowed his patients to go for months or years without
treatment.
syn: notorious   *ant: respectable*

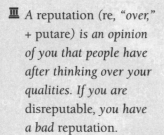
A reputation (re, "over," + putare) is an opinion of you that people have after thinking over your qualities. If you are disreputable, you have a bad reputation.

NOTA
Latin NOTARE, NOTATUM, "to note"

CONNOTATION   (kän ə tā´ shən)   *n.*   an image or idea associated with a word
L. *con*, "together, with" + *notatum* = *noted with*
I fully understand the negative *connotation* of the word you used to describe me.
syn: overtone

DENOTATION   (dē nō tā´ shən)   *n.*   the dictionary definition of a word
L. *de*, "down" + *notare* = *noted from*
In order to grasp the *denotation* of the word, I looked it up in several dictionaries.

How are these two words, connotation and denotation, almost opposite to one another, simply because of their Latin prefixes?

ANNOTATE   (an´ ə tāt)   *v.*   to explain or discuss through a note
L. *ad*, "toward" + *notare* = *noted upon*
The difficult book would have attracted more readers if the author had decided to
annotate it.

RATIO
Latin RATIO, "reason"

IRRATIONAL (i rash´ ən əl) *adj.* not based on reason or logic
L. *in*, "not" + *ratio* = *(having) no reason*
As a child, Christopher was teased for his *irrational* fear of water.
syn: illogical   *ant: reasonable*

RATIONALE (rash ə nal´) *n.* a reason for doing something; an explanation
What *rationale* does the author provide for designing the book this way?

RATIONALIZE (rash´ ən əl īz) *v.* to justify; to give a reason for
I tried my best to *rationalize* spending so much money on one piece of furniture.
syn: excuse

SCI
Latin SCIRE, "to know"

CONSCIENTIOUS (kän shē en´ shəs) *adj.* diligent and careful
L. *com*, "with" + *scire* = *in accordance with knowledge*
Rebecca was a *conscientious* student and a leader in several school clubs.
                    ant: careless

UNCONSCIONABLE (un kän´ shə nə bəl) *adj.* not obeying moral laws;
   unscrupulous
L. *un*, "not" + *con*, "with" + *scire* = *not in accordance with knowledge*
The current administration's repeal of environmental laws has been called
unconscionable by many naturalists.
                    ant: principled

PRESCIENT (presh´ ənt) *adj.* showing knowledge of events before they happen
L. *pre*, "in advance" + *scire* = *to know in advance*
The baseball coach made some decisions that now seem amazingly *prescient*.
syn: farsighted

Ⅲ *The verb* rationalize *has a more negative meaning than its noun counterpart,* rationale. *A* rationale *is simply a reason, while* rationalize *means "to make an excuse."*

Ⅲ *It's often been said that great inventors and innovators are geniuses. Thomas Edison realized that life could be more productive if people had some light after sunset. Henry Ford understood that America could be more connected if transportation were made for the individual. Steve Jobs knew that easily obtainable information about everything would revolutionize communication. These men were not* prescient, *but they all recognized a need and found a way to fill it.*

EXERCISES – UNIT SEVENTEEN

Exercise I. Complete the sentence in a way that shows you understand the meaning of the italicized vocabulary word.

1. The historian decided to *annotate* the chapters in his newest book because…

2. Celeste is a *conscientious* student, so she is sure to…

3. Because of her connection to some *disreputable* businessmen, Naya…

4. The *denotation* of the term that you gave was incorrect because…

5. The only *rationale* I could provide for jumping out of the plane was…

6. If Noah *imputes* her mistake to bad manners, it is because he thinks…

7. My grandmother, hearing about the tornado on the radio, took the *prescient* step of…

8. Sometimes people can be offended by the *connotation* of a word even when…

9. Having worked hard on the project, Lara decided to *dispute*…

10. Norah says that because other people need food and medicine, it is *unconscionable* to…

11. Terry *rationalized* his involvement in stealing a copy of the math final by…

12. It seems *irrational* of Harriet to get angry at Morgan for…

Exercise II. Fill in the blank with the best word from the choices below. One word will not be used.

rationale	annotate	dispute	prescient	conscientious

1. A(n) _____ chapter explained some of the medical terms used in the book.

2. My _____ for cutting class and going to the beach was that it was the first really warm day of the year.

3. Fred insisted that the property line ended at the tree, but his neighbor might _____ the claim.

4. Many people later called the police chief _____ for beefing up the force prior to the major crime wave.

Fill in the blank with the best word from the choices below. One word will not be used.

    disreputable   irrational   impute   annotate   conscientious

5.   My father believed that even a(n) _____ man could redeem himself by doing good deeds.

6.   Natasha feels that if she is _____ about doing her job, she will make few mistakes.

7.   Some citizens _____ the rougher winds in our town to the removal of trees that served as wind blocks.

8.   Although I know my fear of spiders is _____, I can't go near them.

Fill in the blank with the best word from the choices below. One word will not be used.

    impute   connotation   rationalize   denotation   unconscionable

9.   The dictionary's _____ of the word surprised me because I'd always thought it had a different meaning.

10.   It can be easy to _____ a bad decision if you do not think about all the consequences.

11.   It was _____ of Dina to injure a man with her car and then leave the scene.

12.   If you know the _____ of that term, you know it is actually a compliment.

Exercise III. Choose the set of words that best completes the sentence.

1.   You may _____ the claim that the quarterback meant to throw the ball too far, but in light of the play's success, the decision seems very _____.
     A. dispute; prescient
     B. rationalize; conscientious
     C. impute; disreputable
     D. dispute; irrational

2.   How can Julian possibly _____ using a word with such a negative _____ to describe this great man?
     A. impute; rationale
     B. dispute; rationale
     C. rationalize; connotation
     D. annotate; denotation

3.   The historian explains his _____ for writing the book both in the introduction and in the chapters he
     _____ with footnotes.
     A. connotation; disputes
     B. rationale; disputes
     C. rationale; annotates
     D. denotation; imputes

4.   One benefit of being a(n) _____ student is never having to do something as _____ as cheating.
     A. prescient; conscientious
     B. irrational; disreputable
     C. conscientious; unconscionable
     D. conscientious; prescient

5.   While I think it is rather _____ to look to the stars for answers, some people _____ all their troubles to
     the constellations.
     A. irrational; impute
     B. conscientious; rationalize
     C. prescient; impute
     D. unconscionable; rationalize

Exercise IV. Complete the sentence by inferring information about the italicized word from its context.

1.   If an expert on the stock market is often called *prescient*, his predictions about financial affairs indicate…

2.   If Sally worries about the *connotation* of a particular word that she used in describing a coworker, she is
     probably afraid that…

3.   If a medical study *imputes* an illness to a popular medicine, the doctors in the study will probably…

**Exercise V. Fill in each blank with the word from the Unit that best completes the sentence, using the root
     we supply as a clue. Then, answer the questions that follow the paragraphs.**

It is difficult to _____ (PUT) the claim that Booker T. Washington was the most influential African American educator of the late 19th and early 20th centuries. In addition to his contributions to educational theory and practice, Washington had a great impact on race relations in the newly emancipated South and was a leading figure in black public affairs from 1895 until his death in 1915. His success is all the more admirable when one considers that he started life as a slave on a Virginia plantation and slowly worked his way into politics, finally rising to international prominence with his founding of the Tuskegee Institute in Alabama (1881).

Washington was a dedicated supporter of industrial education among African Americans. His support of the Tuskegee Institute placed him in a public spotlight, allowing him to address the subject of racial tensions in general. Washington worked hard to convince Southern white employers and governors that Tuskegee offered an education that would keep blacks on the farm and in the trade industries. To prospective Northern donors, particularly new self-made millionaires such as Rockefeller and Carnegie, Washington made a promise to train students in the ways of the Protestant work ethic. To blacks living with little hope of future success, Washington offered the _____ (RATIO) that industrial education could be a means of escape from poverty; it would lead, he told them, to self-employment, land ownership, and even small business ownership. His charismatic nature allowed him to procure some money from the federal government, but it was Northern donations that made the Tuskegee Institute the best-supported black educational institution in the country. His most famous speech was "The Atlanta Compromise Address," delivered before the Cotton States and International Exposition in 1895. The central theme of his speech was racial tolerance: Washington issued an appeal to whites to encourage black progress in economics and education, while remaining "separate as the fingers" on the hand that builds society.

Washington tried to translate his own personal successes into black advancement through the sponsoring of civil rights suits, serving on the boards of Fisk and Howard Universities, and directing charitable contributions to these and other black colleges. Through various speaking tours and personal communications, he tried to gain equal public educational opportunities for African Americans, as well as to reduce racial violence. Unfortunately, these efforts were generally unsuccessful, and the year of Washington's death marked the beginning of the Great Migration from the rural South to the urban North.

It became apparent at this time that whites had gained control over Southern institutions after the Civil War, and that most of them had never wanted equal rights for African Americans. Many blacks began to turn to the more radical leaders of the time, including William Trotter and W. E. B. Du Bois. Nevertheless, Booker T. Washington is still believed to have been a(n) _____ (SCI) thinker: he had an immense effect on the minds of post-war Southerners, and his theories continue to have an impact today.

1. Which of the following best describes the author's intentions in the writing of this essay?
    A. to explain the differences between Booker T. Washington and other prominent African American leaders at the time, such as W. E. B. Du Bois and William Trotter
    B. to argue that the Tuskegee Institute was one of the greatest American colleges of the 19th century
    C. to explain how Booker T. Washington rose to international prominence because of Tuskegee
    D. to describe the lasting contributions Booker T. Washington made toward American civil rights

2. The author discusses all of the following as reasons for Washington's international popularity EXCEPT
    A. the publication of his autobiography.
    B. the creation of the Tuskegee Institute.
    C. his speeches and fundraising efforts.
    D. his ability to bridge the racial gap between whites and blacks.

3. According to the passage, which of the following famous phrases or statements would Booker T. Washington probably use?
    A. "Separate but equal"
    B. "Peace, love, and happiness"
    C. "By any means necessary"
    D. "Life is a lesson I never want to learn."

4. Washington's image of the races being separate fingers on the same hand is an important one. Which of the following statements most accurately describes the meaning of the symbol?
    A. All races originated in the same place, but have become separate from each other.
    B. If races are completely integrated, more can be accomplished.
    C. All races have to work together to accomplish things.
    D. Some races are weaker than others.

Exercise VI. Drawing on your knowledge of roots and words in context, read the following selection and define the italicized words. If you cannot figure out the meaning of the words on your own, look them up in a dictionary. Note that the prefix *re* means "again" and *omni* means "all."

The poet and artist William Blake was *reputed* to sing his poems aloud before writing them down. His friends and family compared his singing to that of the ancient bard who also sang and wrote poems. In fact, Blake writes of the bard in one of his poems, referring to the writer-musician as *omniscient*. However, there is no evidence showing that Blake envisioned himself, like the bard, as all-knowing and all-powerful.

UNIT EIGHTEEN

AES
Greek AESTHESIS, "feeling, perception"

AESTHETIC (es thet´ ik) *adj.* having to do with beauty or order
The statue has an *aesthetic* value that will last far beyond our own time.
syn: artistic

ANESTHETIC (an es thet´ ik) *n.* a substance that causes loss of feeling
G. *an*, "without" + *aesthesis* = *without feeling*
The doctor administered an *anesthetic* before operating on the patient's foot.

PATH
Greek PATHEIN, "to feel"

APATHETIC (ap ə thet´ ik) *adj.* not interested; having no strong emotion toward
G. *a*, "not" + *pathein* = *having no feeling*
The speaker tried to rally the crowd, but most of the people present were *apathetic*.
syn: indifferent

EMPATHY (em´ pə thē) *n.* the sharing of another's emotions
G. *em*, "inside" + *pathos*, "feeling" = *feeling from inside*
Nelly was divided between feeling *empathy* for her boss and concern about her own future at the company.
syn: compassion   *ant: opposition*

PATHOS (pā´ thōs) *n.* the power to evoke great sadness or sympathy
The sheer *pathos* of the opera's final scene left the audience in tears.
syn: pitifulness

ANTIPATHY (an tip´ ə thē) *n.* a hostility or hatred
G. *anti*, "against" + *pathein* = *feeling against*
The fans' *antipathy* for the coach increased when he lost the game.
syn: dislike   *ant: admiration*

*AUNTIE PATTY felt strong ANTIPATHY
towards anyone who cheated at cards.*

III The Greek word aesthesis *means both "sensory perception"—the ability to feel heat or cold, for instance—and "perception of the beautiful."*

III How are the words apathetic, *"not having strong feelings about something," and* pathetic, *"marked by sorrow or sadness," related?*

SENS, SENT
Latin SENTIRE, SENSUM, "to feel; to be aware"

SENTIENT   (sen´shē ənt)   *adj.*   conscious; aware
Do you think there are other *sentient* beings in the universe?
ant: unaware

SENTINEL   (sen´ti nəl)   *n.*   one who watches or guards
L. literally, "one being aware"
George was posted as a *sentinel* over the camp.

SENTIMENT   (sen´tə mənt)   *n.*   a feeling about something
Although Vinnie expressed his sincere love for Sandra, she did not return
the *sentiment*.
syn: attitude

PRESENTIMENT   (prē zent´ə mənt)   *n.*   a feeling about something before it happens
L. *pre,* "before" + *sentire* = *feeling before*
I had an uneasy *presentiment* about the party that evening.
syn: foreboding

> ▥ A sentiment *can be a simple feeling about something; to be* sentimental *is to be too emotional.*

> ▥ *What adjective from the previous lesson is closely related to* presentiment?

TANG, TACT
Latin TANGERE, TACTUM, "to touch"

TANGIBLE   (tan´jə bəl)   *adj.*   able to be grasped or perceived
The rewards of volunteering may not be as *tangible* as a new car or a new house,
but they are just as real.
syn: concrete   *ant: abstract*

TACTILE   (tak´tīl)   *adj.*   pertaining to touch
The poet uses *tactile* imagery to give his reader the feeling of rough boards and
damp sand.

INTACT   (in takt´)   *adj.*   unbroken; whole
L. *in,* "not" + *tactum* = *not touched*
Amazingly, the vase was *intact* even after rolling to the bottom of the hill.
syn: unharmed

EXERCISES - UNIT EIGHTEEN

Exercise I. Complete the sentence in a way that shows you understand the meaning of the italicized vocabulary word.

1. When my sister lost her job, I felt *empathy* for her because...

2. The teacher encouraged *tactile* interaction between the children and their environment by...

3. Once the *anesthetic* was administered, Dan started to...

4. The *sentinel* at the military base looked for...

5. Although he had once expressed *antipathy* for his stepfather, Owen now...

6. The *presentiment* I had about the meeting caused me to...

7. Justin thought the rug had *aesthetic* appeal, but Jeremy thought...

8. Some people argue that humans are the only *sentient* beings because...

9. Alvin found that the results of his hours at the gym were *tangible* when...

10. The *pathos* of the scene in which the girl kneels beside her kitten made me...

11. When he found that the priceless figurine was *intact*, the collector...

12. The *sentiment* expressed by most of the excited fans at the game was...

13. Nicole was *apathetic* about the idea of the dance until...

Exercise II. Fill in the blank with the best word from the choices below. One word will not be used.

pathos   anesthetic   tangible   tactile   sentient

1. The _____ of Chris's situation certainly made me feel pity for him.

2. As _____ beings, we have the power to understand the world around us.

3. The changes the new boss made in the company were both abstract and _____.

4. We explore our environment not only through vision and hearing, but also in a(n) _____ way.

Fill in the blank with the best word from the choices below. One word will not be used.

sentinel	empathy	anesthetic	intact	presentiment

5.   Although I had a(n) _____ of disaster, I stepped onto the plane anyway.

6.   Because Gina has suffered greatly, she can feel _____ for other people in pain.

7.   My arm was bruised but _____, and I walked off the ski slope basically unhurt.

8.   The drug had a(n) _____ effect, and Del began to lose feeling in his leg.

Fill in the blank with the best word from the choices below. One word will not be used.

sentinel	aesthetic	tactile	apathetic	antipathy	sentiment

9.   Drew is anything but _____ about democracy; he has voted in every local, state, and national election for ten years.

10.   The _____ began to shout that he saw the enemy's torches in the distance.

11.   The _____ I had for Kip only increased when he started insulting my friends.

12.   Even though the beautiful old piano doesn't work, it has a(n) _____ value.

13.   They expressed their positive _____ about my new car by asking if they could drive it.

Exercise III. Choose the set of words that best completes the sentence.

1.   William felt some _____ for the artist whose paintings were destroyed, though he had never agreed with her _____ principles.
     A.   presentiment; anesthetic
     B.   antipathy; sentient
     C.   pathos; anesthetic
     D.   empathy; aesthetic

2.   As _____ beings, we are aware of others' emotions; this awareness allows us to feel the _____ of a great tragedy.
     A.   sentient; anesthetic
     B.   aesthetic; antipathy
     C.   sentient; pathos
     D.   tactile; presentiment

3.   The army came out of the first day of battle tired but _____ and posted a _____ to keep guard over the camp that night.
     A.   apathetic; pathos
     B.   intact; sentinel
     C.   sentient; sentiment
     D.   tangible; presentiment

4. The only _____ reward I get from my job as a volunteer painter is a finished canvas, but the work also gives me _____ satisfaction.
   A. tactile; sentient
   B. intact; tactile
   C. tangible; aesthetic
   D. sentient; apathetic

5. Although Sean had had a _____ that the day would go badly, he was not prepared for the _____ directed at him by his coworkers.
   A. pathos; sentinel
   B. sentinel; empathy
   C. presentiment; antipathy
   D. presentiment; sentinel

Exercise IV. Complete the sentence by inferring information about the italicized word from its context.

1. If an architect complains that most modern buildings have no redeeming *aesthetic* value, he probably means that…

2. When Virginia feels *empathy* for Eric, who has just been severely injured in a car accident, it is probably because…

3. If Oliver explains to you that the rewards of gardening are *tangible*, he probably means that…

Exercise V. Fill in each blank with the word from the Unit that best completes the sentence, using the root we supply as a clue. Then, answer the questions that follow the paragraphs.

In 1981, out of deep _____ (PATH) for the many children who were too poor to afford adequate athletic training and equipment, three-time Olympic gold medalist Wilma Rudolph started the Wilma Rudolph Foundation. The purpose of the organization was to help underprivileged young athletes get the resources and assistance they needed to overcome the numerous obstacles that severe poverty and racism presented. Once again, Rudolph proved that she was firmly determined to reduce or eliminate these obstacles wherever she found them.

Wilma Rudolph had really been set on the path toward the Foundation when she was four years old. One of many children in an impoverished household, she was stricken with a debilitating disease that was later diagnosed as polio, and one of her legs became almost useless as a result. Nonetheless, with the help of her family, she was able to walk almost normally by the age of nine and was soon playing basketball with her brother. In high school, she had to struggle to gain recognition for her talent as an athlete. The segregated school system allocated few of its resources to all-black schools, and Rudolph's school had little equipment or money to participate in competitions. Luckily, Rudolph's talent came to the attention of Ed Temple, the track coach at Tennessee State University. Rudolph eventually became a track star at Tennessee State and then an Olympic medalist on a team coached by Temple. Her gold medal was a(n) _____ (TANG) reward for all of her struggles over the years.

Rudolph was welcomed home from the Olympics to Clarksville, Tennessee, with an enormous parade. At the time, her town was still mostly segregated, and the governor of Tennessee, an ardent segregationist himself, indicated that blacks and whites would be separated during the parade. Rudolph declared that she would not be a part of a segregated celebration. While this stance no doubt earned her the _____ (PATH) of many devotees of segregation, she stood firm, and by her determination furthered the advancement of civil rights in America. In fact, the parade that was held was the first integrated event in Clarksville's history.

Her own experiences with poverty and racial injustice made Wilma Rudolph all the more determined not only to succeed herself, but also to help others succeed. Her primary objective after the Olympics was not stardom, but nurturing athletic talent where it might otherwise not have had the opportunity to develop. After all, she herself had been helped along by people who saw how much she loved to run and knew how to turn her passion into a career.

Rudolph's former coach, Ed Temple, once said about her that she had done more for the United States than she had ever been compensated for. Surely the athletes who grew up in awe of Rudolph's talent and grace would echo this _____ (SENT). Rudolph died in 1994.

1. Why does the author mention the Wilma Rudolph Foundation?
    A. as a way of demonstrating Rudolph's desire to help others overcome poverty
    B. as a way of proving that Rudolph was strongly opposed to racism
    C. as a way of explaining Rudolph's influence on later athletes
    D. as a way of making clear Rudolph's determination to learn to walk

2. Why, according to the author, was Rudolph's success unlikely to occur?
    A. because Rudolph and Temple were from different parts of the country
    B. because Rudolph came from a poor school with few resources
    C. because Rudolph was involved in an accident at an early age
    D. because Rudolph was unaware of the opportunities awaiting athletes

3. What did Rudolph's gold medal provide for her?
    A. a reason to continue as an athlete
    B. a symbol of the evils of segregation
    C. a solid, real prize for her long struggle
    D. a solution to the problem of poverty

Exercise VI. Drawing on your knowledge of roots and words in context, read the following selection and define the italicized words. If you cannot figure out the meaning of the words on your own, look them up in a dictionary. Note that the suffix *as* (from *ad*) means "toward."

Esther looked out her window when she heard the *pathetic* cries of a baby bird hopping on the ground. She noticed that the bird was alone, and it looked as if it was too small to fly, so she decided to give it some food. Raising her window, she tossed out some birdseed, hoping the bird would eat it, which it did. That must have been enough because the tiny bird, as if giving its *assent*, began to chirp. The next instant, its mother appeared, and after eating some food itself, the two flew off together.

UNIT NINETEEN

QUIS
Latin QUAERERE, QUISITUM, "to ask; to seek; to demand"

INQUISITIVE (in kwiz´ ə tiv) *adj.* curious; asking many questions
L. *in*, "in" + *quisitum = seeking into*
Being a somewhat *inquisitive* child, Marian was inclined to ask questions that
were difficult to answer.
ant: uninterested

ACQUISITIVE (ə kwiz´ ə tiv) *adj.* seeking to get things; greedy
L. *ad*, "toward" + *quisitum = seeking toward*
The property was purchased by an *acquisitive* businesswoman who already owned
much of the surrounding land.
syn: demanding   *ant: generous*

REQUISITION (re kwə zish´ən) *n.* 1. the act of ordering or demanding something
                               v. 2. to make a request or demand
L. *re*, "again" + *quisitum = to demand again*
1. The army issued another *requisition* for backup troops and food supplies.
2. The lieutenant had *requisitioned* several horses for backup troops and food
   supplies.

SPOND, SPOUSE
Latin SPONDERE, SPONSUM, "to pledge; to show support for"

ESPOUSE (e spouz´) *v.* to support; to pledge support to
Although he *espouses* the right of free speech, Kenneth doesn't like to listen to me.
syn: advocate   *ant: criticize*

CORRESPOND (kär ə spänd´) *v.* to be similar to; to compare to
L. *con*, "together, with" + *spondere = to support back with*
The scientist showed us how a bone in the dolphin *corresponded* to a bone in the
human.
syn: match   *ant: differ*

DESPONDENT (dəs pän´ dənt) *adj.* lacking all hope
L. *de*, "down" + *spondere = having pledged away (hope)*
When Leah lost her job and then her house, she
became *despondent*.
syn: despairing   *ant: joyful*

*The DESPONDENT CORRESPONDENT
could not get an interview with the
actress.*

Ⅲ *I have no particular
talent. I am merely
inquisitive.*
—Albert Einstein

Ⅲ *English took the word
espouse from French,
which dropped the "n"
from sponsum and added
an "e" to its beginning.*

ROG
Latin ROGARE, ROGATUM, "to ask; to demand"

INTERROGATE   (in ter´ ə gāt)   *v.*   to formally question
L. *inter*, "between" + *rogare* = *to question between regular intervals*
Though the detectives formally *interrogated* the butler twice, his story remained the same.
syn: examine

DEROGATORY   (dər räg´ ə tôr ē)   *adj.*   insulting; degrading
L. *de*, "down" + *rogare* = *seeking to take down*
Boomer and Buzz, hosts of the morning talk show, were criticized for making *derogatory* comments about a certain political figure.
syn: belittling   *ant: complimentary*

ARROGANT   (ar´ ə gənt)   *adj.*   excessively proud; haughty
L. *ad*, "toward" + *rogare* = *demanding from*
It was *arrogant* of Philip to suggest that he could tutor the rest of the class in math.
syn: conceited   *ant: humble*

ABROGATE   (ab´rə gāt)   *v.*   to cancel; to repeal
L. *ab*, "from" + *rogare* = *to seek away from*
If one country decides to *abrogate* the treaty, the other country will start a war.
syn: abolish   *ant: ratify*

PREC
Latin PREX, PRECIS, "prayer"

PRECARIOUS   (pri kâr´ ē əs)   *adj.*   threatened or unsafe
L. literally, "praying (for one's safety)"
Cindy was in a *precarious* position on the old bridge; no matter which way she stepped, it looked like she would fall.
syn: risky   *ant: safe*

IMPRECATION   (im pri kā´ shən)   *n.*   a curse
L. *in*, "against" + *precis* = *a prayer against*
The holy man called down an *imprecation* upon the murderous king.
                ant: blessing

DEPRECATE   (dep´ rə kāt)   *v.*   to show disapproval of
L. *de*, "off, away" + *precis* = *to pray away from*
Your novel may not be perfect, but you shouldn't *deprecate* the work you have done so far.
syn: belittle   *ant: praise*

III *Money doesn't change men, it merely unmasks them. If a man is naturally selfish or arrogant or greedy, the money brings that out, that's all.*
—Henry Ford

III *To deprecate is literally to "avert disaster by praying to someone"—in a way, "to apologize." From its apologetic overtones, we get the meaning "put (oneself) down" or just "put down."*

EXERCISES - UNIT NINETEEN

Exercise I. Complete the sentence in a way that shows you understand the meaning of the italicized vocabulary word.

1.   If the company issues a *requisition* for pens and paper,...

2.   Although I know you are *despondent* now, eventually you will be...

3.   When Pierre was *interrogated* about the warehouse fire, he...

4.   The strong *imprecation* you directed at me made me feel...

5.   The manager of the office was in a *precarious* position at work because...

6.   When our *inquisitive* puppy, Junie, saw the snapping turtle, she...

7.   It was clear that the oil tycoon was growing more *acquisitive* as the years went by because he...

8.   If you *espouse* principles of kindness and love, you will...

9.   Olivia found the speaker's remarks *derogatory*, but Pam thought...

10.   If the government tried to *abrogate* the Second Amendment, gun owners would surely...

11.   I thought that many things in the new country would *correspond* to things in my homeland, but...

12.   Before you *deprecate* the job of a teacher, you should know that...

13.   The twins' *arrogant* behavior often made their friends...

Exercise II. Fill in the blank with the best word from the choices below. One word will not be used.

inquisitive   despondent   abrogate   precarious   interrogate

1.   Although some people feel it is dangerous to be too _____, others think you should seek knowledge constantly.

2.   The priest found himself in a(n) _____ position; he did not know whom to trust, but he could not keep the information secret.

3.   When France chose to _____ the treaty with Britain, the British were outraged.

4.   I am afraid that if the police decide to _____ me, I will not be able to answer their questions.

Fill in the blank with the best word from the choices below. One word will not be used.

despondent   requisition   espouse   acquisitive   imprecation

5.   If you would stop screaming _____, maybe we could talk like civilized people.

6.   When Trina learned that she would not graduate, she became _____.

7.   The relief organization needed to _____ more food for the hungry refugees.

8.   Marty claims to _____ the founding principles of an independent political party.

Fill in the blank with the best word from the choices below. One word will not be used.

deprecate   acquisitive   interrogate   arrogant   correspond   derogatory

9.   Because of her rather _____ nature, Jill tends to accumulate goods and possessions.

10.   In what many considered a(n) _____ gesture, the senator refused to meet with any members of the committee.

11.   I demanded an apology for a comment I thought was _____.

12.   It was Fred's habit to _____ the achievements of his noble family because he didn't want to seem vain.

13.   My interior decorator said, "These pale blue curtains _____ closely to your wallpaper and sofa."

Exercise III. Choose the set of words that best completes the sentence.

1.   If you keep making such _____ comments about your little sister, you'll make her sad or even _____.
      A. inquisitive; derogatory
      B. derogatory; despondent
      C. inquisitive; precarious
      D. precarious; despondent

2.   The country was in a(n) _____ position, unsure whether to _____ the treaty or not.
      A. despondent; correspond
      B. acquisitive; espouse
      C. precarious; abrogate
      D. derogatory; deprecate

3.   It is hard to see how someone as _____ and conceited as Mr. Thorpe could _____ the principles of modesty and kindness.
      A. despondent; abrogate
      B. arrogant; espouse
      C. acquisitive; deprecate
      D. arrogant; correspond

4.   While doing extra research, the _____ student discovered that words in one language _____ to the words in another.
     A. inquisitive; corresponded
     B. despondent; interrogated
     C. precarious; deprecated
     D. inquisitive; espoused

5.   If you _____ Danny, you can be sure he will get back at you with some unrepeatable _____.
     A. correspond; requisition
     B. deprecate; imprecation
     C. abrogate; imprecation
     D. interrogate; requisition

Exercise IV. Complete the sentence by inferring information about the italicized word from its context.

1.   If someone described Mark as *acquisitive*, you might expect to see Mark constantly…

2.   When a nation *abrogates* a treaty, another nation under the treaty will probably…

3.   If someone who knows about a crime is *interrogated,* he or she will probably…

Exercise V. Fill in each blank with the word from the Unit that best completes the sentence, using the root we supply as a clue. Then, answer the questions that follow the paragraphs.

In recent years, a controversial theory has gained a following among Shakespearean scholars: that Edward de Vere, 17th Earl of Oxford and a learned court insider during the Elizabethan period, was the true author of the plays and sonnets generally attributed to William Shakespeare. People who _____ (SPOUSE) this view claim that "Shakespeare" was merely a clever pen name, and that de Vere assumed the identity of an English commoner from Stratford in order to publish his politically scandalous writings. Their case was first argued by Charlton Ogburn in his book *The Mysterious William Shakespeare*.

Ogburn laid out a comprehensive argument based mainly on Shakespeare's lineage and education. Shakespeare was the son of a tradesman, and evidence that he received formal instruction is inconclusive. History records that he was a sometime actor and occasional real estate investor. His death seemed to go unnoticed and was not marked by the notices in the press that one would expect for a great writer.

Furthermore, his will mentions no writings, and there is no evidence that he ever owned a book. How, supporters of Ogburn inquire, can anyone reconcile the brilliance of the writings with such an obscure existence?

The life of Edward de Vere, however, really does seem to _____ (SPOND) to the range of knowledge reflected in the work of Shakespeare. De Vere came from a wealthy family and was England's highest-ranking earl. He was a poet, an adventurer, and a court regular; his extensive education and knowledge of the world would have prepared him exceedingly well for a second career as a playwright and sonneteer. In addition, the de Vere theorists have a ready motive for their author-in-disguise: he wanted to publish politically sensitive material, but would have been exiled or worse for doing so openly.

Ogburn's book made an immediate impact on scholars of English literature. It set the stage for various debates and mock trials, including one before three US Supreme Court justices. Although the final "trial" ended with a decision in favor of the original Shakespeare, the controversy continues. Those who believe de Vere was Shakespeare must accept an elaborate hoax and a conspiracy of silence, while those who side with the man from Stratford-upon-Avon must lean heavily on the miraculous power of human creativity.

1. Which of the following is NOT an argument made by Ogburn's supporters?
   A. The real Shakespeare "was the son of a tradesman" and was unlikely to gain literary fame.
   B. Shakespeare and de Vere were partners in a "conspiracy of silence."
   C. De Vere "would have been exiled or worse," so he used an alias to publish his opinions.
   D. De Vere, unlike Shakespeare, had money and "was England's highest-ranking earl."

2. What is the purpose of the first paragraph?
   A. to introduce the controversy surrounding Shakespeare and de Vere
   B. to argue that de Vere took the name "Shakespeare" and assumed the identity of a commoner
   C. to describe the Shakespearean scholars who are involved in the de Vere controversy
   D. to explain why de Vere is a likely candidate for the real Shakespeare

3. Why is the sentence "His death seemed to go unnoticed and was not marked by the notices in the press that one would expect for a great writer" included in the passage?
   A. The author is explaining the relationship of Edward de Vere to the person we know as Shakespeare.
   B. The author is supplying one reason not to believe that Shakespeare actually wrote the plays.
   C. The author is detailing why de Vere might have attempted to disguise himself as a playwright.
   D. The author is explaining why he or she feels that Shakespeare came from a middle-class family.

Exercise VI. Drawing on your knowledge of roots and words in context, read the following selection and define the italicized words. If you cannot figure out the meaning of the words on your own, look them up in a dictionary. Note that the prefix *re* means "back" and *pre* means "before."

During the initial hearing, Judge Samuel Larson listened to the *respondent's* testimony and the evidence she gave to support her case. When she was through, Judge Larson asked the person who had brought charges against the woman to provide proof of her guilt. The man couldn't produce any solid evidence, and it was clear that he had been lying. As it was the judge's *prerogative*, he immediately dismissed the case and fined the man for his false accusations.

UNIT TWENTY

MON
Latin MONERE, MONITUM, "to warn"

ADMONITION (ad mə nish´ən) *n.* a gentle scolding
L. *ad*, "toward" + *monitum = warning toward*
The judge released me with the *admonition* to stay away from people who got me into trouble.
syn: chiding

PREMONITION (pre mə nish´ən) *n.* a vision; a warning of something before it
    happens
L. *pre*, "before" + *monitum = warning before*
I had a *premonition* that the day would go badly as soon as I woke up.
syn: presentiment

What admonition *and* premonition *have in common is their Latin root* monere. *A* premonition *might make a person feel uneasy about what is to come, but an* admonition *might make a person uneasy about not repeating the thing that caused him or her to receive a warning in the first place.*

CONSIL
Latin CONCILIARE, "to bring together"
Latin CONSILIUM, "advice"

COUNSEL (koun´səl) *v.* 1. to advise; to make a suggestion to
                          n. 2. advice
1. The farmer's brother *counseled* him to sell the farm and move to the city.
syn: encourage   *ant: discourage*
2. The lottery winners will seek the *counsel* of a lawyer before revealing their
    identities.

CONCILIATORY (kən sil´ ē ə tôr ē) *adj.* intended to lessen another's anger
In a *conciliatory* gesture, Judith offered to give her medal to her opponent.
syn: appeasing   *ant: defiant, aggressive*

RECONCILE (rek´ən sīl) *v.* to bring back into agreement
L. *re*, "back" + *consiliare = to bring back together*
Dawn tried to *reconcile* two of her friends, who were fighting.
syn: harmonize   *ant: upset*

The Latin word conciliare *means "to call together, to bring to assembly." In Rome, a group that was called together (the Senate, for instance) could provide* consilium, *or advice, to a leader.*

The warring CROCODILES finally RECONCILED.

CAUT
Latin CAVEO, CAUTUM, "to be careful"

PRECAUTION (prē kô´ shən) *n.* an action taken against danger ahead of time
L. *pre*, "before" + *cautum* = *to be careful before*
I have never been in an accident, but I always wear my seatbelt as a *precaution*.

CAUTIOUS (kô´ shəs) *adj.* careful not to get into danger
After a series of major financial scandals, investors are usually more *cautious*.
syn: prudent

CAUTIONARY (kô´ shən e rē) *adj.* intended to serve as a warning
The minister told us a *cautionary* tale about the dangers of vanity.

SUAD
Latin SUADERE, SUASUM, "to advise"

DISSUADE (dis wād´) *v.* to convince one not to do something
L. *dis*, "not" + *suasum* = *to advise not to*
No matter how I tried, I could not *dissuade* Vince from going into the haunted house.
syn: discourage   *ant: persuade*

PERSUASION (pər swā´ zhen) *n.* a habit or type
I certainly know people who love all kinds of sports, although I am not of that *persuasion*.
syn: camp

⬛ *The Latin phrase* caveat emptor *means "let the buyer beware"; a* caveat *is a warning.*

⬛ *At one time, the noun* persuasion *meant "the religion one is* persuaded *to believe in." Eventually, it lost its connection with religion and came to mean "type" or "kind."*

EXERCISES - UNIT TWENTY

Exercise I. Complete the sentence in a way that shows you understand the meaning of the italicized vocabulary word.

1.   If Frank, whom Lisa does not trust, *counsels* Lisa to take a job, Lisa will probably…

2.   Connie, who was usually on the *cautious* side, surprised us by…

3.   One *admonition* that mothers often issue to their children is…

4.   When Irene had an unpleasant *premonition* about the trip, she decided to…

5.   In order to *reconcile* with my sisters, whom I had been fighting with for months, I…

6.   As a *precaution*, the firefighters always…

7.   As a *conciliatory* act toward his political opponent, Governor Hodges…

8.   *Cautionary* signs on the sides of the roads warned…

9.   The only way to *dissuade* a very stubborn person from doing something is to…

10.   Most of the people at the party were of the *persuasion* that likes classical music, but some…

Exercise II. Fill in the blank with the best word from the choices below. One word will not be used.

admonition   dissuade   conciliatory   counsel

1.   I could not _____ Parker from entering the beauty contest, no matter how hard I tried.

2.   Do you think Deanna's gift of her favorite toy to KC was a(n) _____ act, meant to win back her brother's favor?

3.   Having given Lionel a(n) _____ about being more careful, the teacher let him go.

Fill in the blank with the best word from the choices below. One word will not be used.

precaution   counsel   premonition   cautious   reconcile

4.   If you _____ Reed to seek help with his homework, he will probably take your advice.

5.   I had a terrible _____ and decided to stay home instead of going to work.

6.   Be _____ when it comes to your personal finances; try to save money.

7.   If you can _____ these two opinions, which are so different, I will be amazed.

Fill in the blank with the best word from the choices below. One word will not be used.

cautionary   persuasion   precaution   reconcile

8.   As a _____, always wear a helmet when you ride your bike.

9.   I am of the _____ that likes to stay in and read books; my sister is the sort of person who likes to go to parties and movies.

10. The popular, _____ song about not judging people made me and my friends rethink our values.

Exercise III. Choose the set of words that best completes the sentence.

1.   If you are of the _____ that does not like to take _____, be prepared for bad things to happen.
     A. persuasion; precautions
     B. precaution; persuasions
     C. admonition; counsel
     D. counsel; admonition

2.   The _____ tale warned that if you don't try to _____ with your enemies, everyone will suffer.
     A. conciliatory; dissuade
     B. cautionary; reconcile
     C. cautious; dissuade
     D. cautionary; counsel

3.   Although I cannot _____ you from getting back at the man who took your money, at least I can _____ you to be extremely careful.
     A. reconcile; dissuade
     B. reconcile; counsel
     C. dissuade; reconcile
     D. dissuade; counsel

4.   Instead of being _____ after our fight, Hannah gave me a(n) _____ about not being so bossy.
     A. cautionary; counsel
     B. conciliatory; admonition
     C. cautious; persuasion
     D. conciliatory; persuasion

5.   After I had a terrible _____ about a car crash, I started being more _____ on the roads.
     A. admonition; cautious
     B. premonition; counseled
     C. premonition; cautious
     D. admonition; conciliatory

Exercise IV. Complete the sentence by inferring information about the italicized word from its context.

1.   If your best friend *counsels* you to accept an offer, you will likely...

2.   If you try to *reconcile* two friends, another will assume they have been...

3.   A person usually gives an *admonition* to another person who has...

Exercise V. Fill in each blank with the word from the Unit that best completes the sentence, using the root we supply as a clue. Then, answer the questions that follow the paragraphs.

Inspired by her own difficulties, Eleanor Roosevelt carried on a long heritage of political activism. Her early education helped to foster a deep interest in social causes, especially those involving women, the poor, and all underprivileged people. She was an early member of the National Consumers League, striving for improvement of working conditions for women. As a young woman of 21, against the _____ (CAUT) advice of her future mother-in-law, she became the wife of Franklin Delano Roosevelt. This marriage would provide Eleanor with her greatest opportunities to bring about political change.

During the First World War, Eleanor was active in many volunteer organizations, including the Red Cross. Upon her husband's appointment to President Woodrow Wilson's Cabinet, Eleanor took advantage of the opportunity to lead the cause for more social reform and became more involved in politics. After Franklin Roosevelt lost his bid for the vice presidency in 1920 and was diagnosed with polio, Eleanor threw herself into efforts for the causes she supported, including women's independence. She held office in the League of Women Voters and the Democratic Committee of New York. She spent considerable time campaigning for Democratic candidates across New York State, even, at one point, trying to _____ (SUAD) people from voting for her Republican cousin Theodore Roosevelt, Jr. in his bid for governor.

She championed the cause of women workers, African Americans, writers, scholars, artists, and actors. The first white resident in Washington, D.C., to join the NAACP, she resigned from the Daughters of the American Revolution when the organization failed to grant membership to renowned black singer Marian Anderson. She fought against racial discrimination, comparing segregation and racism in America to fascism abroad. Her crusade for an end to discrimination even made her a target of the Ku Klux Klan.

During World War II, Eleanor visited troops in Europe and held a position in the Office of Civil Defense. She was an independent journalist, a gifted public speaker, a magazine columnist, and a beloved radio personality. However, she and Franklin could not _____ (CONSIL) their opposing views about a woman's place in society. At her husband's request, she reluctantly gave up many of the activities in which she was involved.

After Franklin's death, Eleanor remained loyal to liberal causes that were not always supported by the governing administration. However, President Harry Truman, despite the fact that her views differed from his own, appointed Roosevelt to the post of US Representative to the United Nations. She led the Human Rights Commission for five years, and later, by appointment of President John Kennedy, led the President's Commission on the Status of Women.

Eleanor Roosevelt, a champion of equality and peace, died in 1962.

1. Which of the following conclusions can be logically drawn from the passage?
   A. Franklin Roosevelt approved of all his wife's activities.
   B. Eleanor Roosevelt was an advocate of social causes.
   C. Studying can make a woman a political candidate.
   D. Presidents like women to be involved in politics.

2. Which of the following would be the best title for the passage?
   A. Eleanor Roosevelt's Change of Heart
   B. A President's Wife Speaks Out
   C. A First Lady's Activism
   D. How to Succeed as a Woman

3. From the passage, you can infer that Eleanor Roosevelt did not want to surrender her leadership roles in certain organizations because
   A. she thought that staying at home would be dangerous.
   B. she enjoyed working for her husband.
   C. she was jealous of her husband's position.
   D. she thought she would be unable to accomplish her goals.

Exercise VI. Drawing on your knowledge of roots and words in context, read the following selection and define the italicized words. If you cannot figure out the meaning of the words on your own, look them up in a dictionary. Note that the prefix _in_ means "not."

The city commissioners met at the conference room to discuss the building of a new statue for the park. After deciding on a _monument_ in honor of prisoners of war, they invited Mr. Hadley into the room. Mr. Hadley was an environmental consultant who came to discuss the pollution risks of construction near the park's lake. He had often warned the commissioners not to be _incautious_ when it came to the environment.

UNIT TWENTY-ONE

GUST
Latin GUSTUS, "taste"

GUSTO (gus´tō) *n.* enthusiastic enjoyment
The hungry children dug into the delicious spaghetti with great *gusto*.
syn: relish   *ant: dislike*

GUSTATORY (gus´tə tôr ē) *adj.* having to do with the sense of taste
Gene thanked the waiter for the best *gustatory* experience of his life.

SIP, SAP
Latin SAPERE, "to taste"

INSIPID (in si´pəd) *adj.* dull; uninteresting
L. *in*, "not" + *sapere* = having *no taste*
Wendy quickly tired of her sister's *insipid* conversation.
syn: colorless   *ant: intriguing*

SAPIENT (sā´pē ənt) *adj.* having knowledge; wise
Human beings have long thought themselves the only *sapient* beings on planet Earth.
syn: conscious   *ant: unthinking*

AV
Latin AVERE, "to crave; to desire"

AVID (a´vəd) *adj.* enthusiastic; eager
Stan was such an *avid* fan of the team that he called in sick rather than miss the big game.
syn: devoted   *ant: uninterested*

AVARICE (a´və rəs) *n.* a desire for wealth; greed
Nelson's *avarice* led him to make risky decisions on behalf of the company.

The verb sapere *was often used by Roman authors to mean not only "taste," but "have good taste" or "be wise." This second meaning is the one that has influenced our English words. It is why, for example, the name of the species to which human beings belong is* Homo Sapiens—*literally, "Wise Man."*

Poverty wants some things, Luxury many things, Avarice all *things.*
—Benjamin Franklin

BIB
Latin BIBERE, "to drink"

IMBIBE   (im bīb´)   *v.*   to drink; to soak up
L. *in*, "into" + *bibere* = *to drink in*
Spanish merchants, having *imbibed* the culture of their Middle Eastern trading partners, brought new customs back to Spain.
syn: absorb

BIBULOUS   (bi´ byə ləs)   *adj.*   drunken
When I asked how the party was going, Chuck gave me a *bibulous* grin.

GLUT
Latin GLUTTIRE, "to devour"

GLUT   (glut)   *n.*   too much of something; an oversupply
The *glut* of similar-sounding songs on the radio station drove listeners to change the channel.

GLUTTON   (glu´ tən)   *n.*   one who wants or takes too much (especially food or drink)
Anyone who eats as much turkey as Sheila did is a *glutton* in my opinion.

Max was an incredible GLUTTON for MUTTON.

PALAT
Latin PALATUM, "palate"

PALATE   (pa´ lət)   *n.*   a taste or liking
Although many people like the music of Mozart, it does not suit my *palate*.
syn: appetite

PALATABLE   (pa´ lə tə bəl)   *adj.*   acceptable; satisfactory
I found the actor's impressions *palatable*, but I wouldn't recommend him for any awards.
syn: tolerable   *ant: unbearable*

▥ *Medieval religious beliefs stated that seven sins were particularly terrible; these were therefore called the seven "deadly sins." Avarice and gluttony are two; the others are wrath, sloth, pride, lust, and envy.*

▥ *Do not confuse these three words, which is easy to do: Palate, meaning "taste"; Palette, the artist's board used for mixing paint; and Pallet, which is a wooden platform used for storage.*

EXERCISES - UNIT TWENTY-ONE

Exercise I. Complete the sentence in a way that shows you understand the meaning of the italicized vocabulary word.

1. Edgar believes that *sapient* organisms may inhabit distant planets because...

2. Because Doreen did not find the professor's ideas *palatable*, she...

3. Tired of the *insipid* dialogue in the movie, I decided to...

4. Marc was an *avid* chess player, so he often...

5. Because Frank calls the Hot Dog Shack "a *gustatory* house of horrors,"...

6. My aunt has a very limited *palate* when it comes to sports; she only...

7. When the freshwater plants *imbibed* the salty water, they...

8. Because of the *glut* of crops on the market this season, the farmers saw...

9. When asked about her years abroad, Samantha remembers *bibulous* evenings that often ended in...

10. Terrence ate his lima beans with unusual *gusto* because...

11. If I let my little brother, a *glutton* by nature, see the new box of cookies,...

12. The *avarice* displayed by the leaders of the country is especially shameful because...

Exercise II. Fill in the blank with the best word from the choices below. One word will not be used.

gusto   avarice   sapient   avid   bibulous

1. The personal ad read, "Looking for another _____ golfer to share many hours on the golf course."

2. Jay is a(n) _____ fellow who can often be found cheerfully ordering a round of drinks for a group of complete strangers.

3. Lisa found few friends who matched her intellectual ability, and she often despaired of ever coming across anyone _____.

4. After the pep talk, the basketball players went back to their work with new _____.

Fill in the blank with the best word from the choices below. One word will not be used.

glut   imbibe   palatable   gustatory   insipid

5.   I remember so much about Paris—the sights, the sounds, and especially the _____ pleasures.

6.   The hiring manager complained that a(n) _____ of workers made it difficult to find jobs for everyone.

7.   Imagine my surprise when my date turned out to be exciting and intelligent rather than a(n) _____ drone.

8.   Because of television, citizens of one country may now _____ freely of the cultures of another.

Fill in the blank with the best word from the choices below. One word will not be used.

sapient   glutton   palate   avarice   palatable

9.   The most important vow a monk takes involves giving up the pleasures of the world, so Brother John's _____ was confusing to everyone.

10.   Are the candidates' speeches _____ to you, or do you find them disagreeable?

11.   I was horrified to hear the mistress of the orphanage call the rail-thin child a(n) _____.

12.   Teresa traveled the world to develop her _____ and see what she liked.

Exercise III. Choose the set of words that best completes the sentence.

1.   Shonda, a(n) _____ reader since childhood, devoured the author's new book with great _____.
   A.   palatable; gusto
   B.   avid; avarice
   C.   gustatory; glut
   D.   avid; gusto

2.   The count promises _____ delights and _____ hilarity at his next grand party.
   A.   bibulous; sapient
   B.   gustatory; bibulous
   C.   palatable; sapient
   D.   gustatory; insipid

3. The student had outgrown her teacher and no longer found his lectures _____; they were so _____ and
    uninspiring that she often fell asleep in class.
    A. gustatory; palatable
    B. bibulous; avid
    C. palatable; insipid
    D. sapient; avid

4. Even the most _____ creatures among us must develop a(n) _____ for certain areas of knowledge.
    A. palatable; glut
    B. sapient; palate
    C. gluttonous; avarice
    D. bibulous; glutton

5. Despite the _____ John displayed as a banker, he was not a(n) _____ at the dinner table.
    A. gusto; palate
    B. glut; avarice
    C. avarice; glutton
    D. palate; gusto

Exercise IV. Complete the sentence by inferring information about the italicized word from its context.

1. Faced with another day of *insipid* chatter in the lounge, Peter may choose to...

2. If Avery receives a *glut* of presents for her birthday, people might think...

3. Because I told Sarah's new boyfriend that she is an *avid* swimmer, he...

Exercise V. Fill in each blank with the word from the Unit that best completes the sentence, using the root we supply as a clue. Then, answer the questions that follow the paragraphs.

Much of Frank Sinatra's enduring fame can be traced to one movie: *From Here to Eternity*. Without this film, many cultural critics agree that Sinatra would probably have disappeared from the spotlight after a career as a minor actor and unique singer of romantic ballads.

In this 1953 picture set in pre-World War II Pearl Harbor, Sinatra plays Angelo Maggio, an underdog hero who resists the bullying of his sergeant, James Judson, (played by Academy Award-winner Ernest Borgnine), but eventually pays a terrible price. After several run-ins with the sergeant, whom he calls "Fatso," Maggio is arrested by military police for leaving the base without permission. His warden during the time of imprisonment is none other than Judson, who spends several days beating him severely. Maggio escapes the prison and, with his dying breath, reveals his murderer to his fellow soldier and friend, Robert Prewitt (played by

Montgomery Clift). Prewitt avenges Maggio's murder in a way that further complicates the tragedy.

At the time *From Here to Eternity* came out, Sinatra's film and music careers both looked uncertain. He had been dropped from a major record label a year before; even previously _____ (AV) fans now considered him a has-been. However, Sinatra pleaded with the film studio to give him a chance, even agreeing to accept a salary much lower than the going rate for actors starring in a major motion picture, and he was chosen for the role. The decision saved his career and resulted in a beloved movie. The sincerity with which Sinatra delivered the role of Maggio won back old fans and earned him new ones. Maggio is an innocent character who likes to joke around, someone who takes to life with great _____ (GUST) despite the war beginning all around him. In order to play the part, Sinatra had to bring to life the combination of childish vulnerability and stubborn heroism that makes the character of Maggio so sympathetic. The part won Sinatra an Oscar for Best Supporting Actor in 1954.

Some critics of Sinatra's work in *From Here to Eternity* complain that he is not actually acting, but playing a role not far removed from his own personality. Maggio, like Sinatra, is a funny, charming character of Italian ancestry. Other critics who disliked the film claimed that the performance is overblown and melodramatic: Maggio, they say, moves too quickly from being irritatingly cheerful to unconvincingly pathetic. For example, he dies a clichéd and overly emotional death in his best friend's arms. Nevertheless, the film is now considered a classic. Despite the opinions of those who find Sinatra's acting barely _____ (PALAT), or even unwatchable, moviegoers return to it again and again.

1.   Based on the passage, you can logically infer that a Sinatra fan would probably disagree most with which of the following statements?
      A. Playing Maggio was a decision that was perfect for Sinatra.
      B. *From Here to Eternity* gave Sinatra the career he deserved.
      C. Singing was where Sinatra really excelled and showed his talent.
      D. Without playing Maggio, Sinatra never would have been a star.

2.   What would be considered the best point made in the third paragraph?
      A. Even people who have talent find it difficult to overcome obstacles.
      B. Taking advantage of opportunities may not lead to success.
      C. Through sheer willpower, a person can obtain a second chance in life.
      D. Some people can achieve their dreams without even trying much.

3.   The author wrote the passage in a form that
      A. moves chronologically through Sinatra's career.
      B. presents varied opinions about the movie.
      C. shows a definite bias that favors Sinatra.
      D. presents a theory and then contradicts it.

Exercise VI. Drawing on your knowledge of roots and words in context, read the following selection and define the italicized words. If you cannot figure out the meaning of the words on your own, look them up in a dictionary.

Although the doctor had warned Kendra that the medicine might interfere with *gustation*, she was unprepared for what occurred. Dining became a chore, rather than a pleasure; even holidays were less enjoyable because she was unable to really share the meals with her family. The *sapor* not only of food, but of life eluded her.

UNIT TWENTY-TWO

RANC
Latin RANCERE, "to stink"

RANCID (ran´ səd) *adj.* rotten; spoiled
After the power outage, we were forced to throw out three bottles of *rancid* milk.
syn: soured   *ant: fresh*

RANCOR (ran´ kər) *n.* bitterness; hostility
The *rancor* between the two businesses was only deepened by disagreement over the new law.
syn: enmity   *ant: friendliness*

III *The Spanish term* olla podrida, *which literally means "rotten pot," refers to a stew of meat and vegetables; it can also mean a mishmash of ideas.* Podrida *comes from* putris. *The French word* potpourri *is a translation of* olla podrida.

PUTR
Latin PUTRIS, "rotten"

PUTREFY (pū´ trə fī) *v.* to rot; to decompose
The soldiers had to bury the bodies quickly so that they would not *putrefy* in the hot sun.

PUTRID (pū´ trəd) *adj.* rotten; suggesting decomposition
The walls of the cave were covered with slime, and the air was filled with the stench of something *putrid*.
syn: rancid

III *While* stagnant *and* stagnate *literally apply to standing bodies of water, they may also be used figuratively. For example, a stagnant economy could use some stirring up.*

STAGN
Latin STAGNARE, "to stagnate; to form a pool of standing water"

STAGNANT (stag´ nənt) *adj.* unhealthy because of lack of movement
The *stagnant* air of the marsh was blamed for many illnesses.
syn: sluggish   *ant: invigorating*

STAGNATE (stag´ nāt) *v.* to stop moving or growing; to become unhealthy because of lack of movement
Marcia was afraid that she would *stagnate* in the unchallenging atmosphere of the office, but she actually found many opportunities to be creative.
syn: vegetate

ODOR
Latin ODOR, "smell"

MALODOROUS (mal ō´ də rəs) *adj.* foul-smelling
L. *malus*, "bad" + *odor* = *bad-smelling*
Joelle could hardly bear to be in the room when her father opened the package of *malodorous* cheese.

ODORIFEROUS (ō də ri´ fə rəs) *adj.* giving off an odor
L. *odor* + *ferre*, "to bear; to carry" = *odor-bearing*
The herbal medicine smells strong because it is made of a combination of *odoriferous* plants.

OL
Latin OLERE, "to smell"

OLFACTORY (ōl fak´ tə rē) *adj.* having to do with the sense of smell
L. *olere* + *facere*, "to make or do" = *ability to smell*
The *olfactory* ability of the average bloodhound makes it far better than a human being at following a scent.

The OLD FACTORY produced so much gas that it hurt my OLFACTORY nerve.

REDOLENT (re´ də lənt) *adj.* suggesting; carrying the hint of
L. *re*, "back" + *olere* = *bringing the odor back*
I found the poet's essays *redolent* of the first days of the revolution.
syn: reminiscent

FET
Latin FETERE, "to stink"

FETID (fe´ təd) *adj.* having an unpleasant smell
The *fetid* stench of rotting fish rose from the polluted stream.

Ⅲ There is a disease, caused by a nerve or brain problem, called anosmia, which involves the loss of olfactory senses. While it might be a blessing if you were close to a skunk, people who have this problem suffer because all food tastes pretty much the same if you cannot smell.

Ⅲ Asafetida is a flavoring derived from a plant related to the carrot. Its name is a combination of the Persian aza, a name for a kind of tree-sap, and fetidus.

EXERCISES – UNIT TWENTY-TWO

Exercise I. Complete the sentence in a way that shows you understand the meaning of the italicized vocabulary word.

1.   I was surprised when Cheryl called the cookies *malodorous* because…

2.   The pool in the deserted town started to *stagnate* when…

3.   The atmosphere on the small town's main street was *redolent* of…

4.   The ingredients in the compost pile started to *putrefy* after…

5.   When the patient's *olfactory* nerve was injured, he…

6.   Because the dangerous substance is both strongly colored and *odoriferous*…

7.   The first camper who noticed the *rancid* vegetables…

8.   Flies circled the *putrid* heap of scraps, making me feel…

9.   The green, *stagnant* surface of the brook led me to believe that…

10.   Trying to avoid the *rancor* that had filled their first meeting, the two groups…

11.   Dawn believed that the *fetid* substance she had developed for her science fair project made the judges…

Exercise II. Fill in the blank with the best word from the choices below. One word will not be used.

   putrefy   redolent   rancid   stagnate   malodorous

1.   I was surprised when Suha claimed to find the odor of _____ milk delightful.

2.   Contrary to popular belief, pigs are not _____ creatures.

3.   We hoped our fruit would last for months, but it began to spoil and _____ in the hot, moist air.

4.   Brian was afraid that the water gathered in the sewer would _____ and breed disease.

Fill in the blank with the best word from the choices below. One word will not be used.

redolent   fetid   stagnant   olfactory

5. The doctors specializing in _____ disorders were confused by the patient's inability to smell anything at night.

6. Anna said that the scuffle in the street was hardly _____ of the major brawls that had rocked the town years before.

7. When peeled, the fruit has a _____ odor, like that of old socks.

Fill in the blank with the best word from the choices below. One word will not be used.

fetid   odoriferous   putrid   rancor   stagnant

8. Scientists studying decomposition delight in _____ matter that other people find disgusting.

9. Paul showed the _____ he had felt for years when he refused to shake my hand.

10. Our _____ economy seems unable to make any progress no matter what major events occur.

11. Jackson hated having to drink the _____ concoction of vitamins that his mother prepared.

Exercise III. Choose the set of words that best completes the sentence.

1. _____ of the government's long history of internal fighting, the crisis in Congress dragged on; some said the _____ between senators would soon grow worse.
    A. Malodorous; rancor
    B. Olfactory; rancor
    C. Putrid; rancor
    D. Redolent; rancor

2. As she approached the silent, _____ brook, Lakshmi was struck by the smell of something unimaginably _____.
    A. putrid; olfactory
    B. fetid; stagnant
    C. stagnant; putrid
    D. malodorous; olfactory

3.   "What a(n) _____ candle," sniffed Herman. "It smells like some horrible vegetable has _____ in here."
   A. putrid; stagnated
   B. malodorous; putrefied
   C. olfactory; putrefied
   D. putrid; stagnated

4.   In a study of human _____ responses, subjects smelled both fresh and _____ salad dressing.
   A. malodorous; putrid
   B. stagnant; fetid
   C. putrid; stagnant
   D. olfactory; rancid

5.   When allowed to _____, the canal filled with _____ seaweed that could be smelled for miles.
   A. stagnate; fetid
   B. putrefy; olfactory
   C. putrefy; stagnant
   D. stagnate; olfactory

Exercise IV. Complete the sentence by inferring information about the italicized word from its context.

1.   When Mariah says that she is *stagnating* in her current job, we can guess that she would like to...

2.   If Gina says that something in the room must be *rancid*, the expression on her face is probably one of...

3.   A book dealing with *olfactory* disorders will probably be filled with pictures of...

Exercise V. Fill in each blank with the word from the Unit that best completes the sentence, using the root we supply as a clue. Then, answer the questions that follow the paragraphs.

In the upcoming *Zombie Night Five*, a group of five teenagers is stalked and gradually eliminated by an evil presence that turns them into the living dead. What seems to be a run-of-the-mill slasher flick turns out, on closer observation, to be an intelligent look at some of America's most important issues.

Take, for example, a scene in which Shelby (played by Greta Reese) manages to escape the zombies by finding her way into a toy store with an unlocked back door. There, to her surprise, she finds Zeke (Elijah Mbembe) and Alice (Darlene Knut) already there; they relate their own stories of near death to her. Arguments arise over what to do. Shelby suggests that they make a mad dash for a store selling religious artifacts on the upper level of the mall. Alice murmurs fatalistically that they would be better off heading

for the _____ (ODOR) dumpsters behind the mall, thereby at least spoiling the zombies' appetites as they are devoured.

The clever humor of the scene is typical of the film, and the actors deliver their lines with perfect timing. However, its larger message about conflicts between religious believers and nonbelievers—the characters move into a dialogue that I won't spoil for you here—is even more skillfully delivered. Regardless of your views on religion, you will appreciate this film's thoughtful consideration of the "great faith divide."

In addition, the film is filled with clever pop-culture references and subtle jabs at the "material American" of our time. The setting of the film in the mall is no accident; stores that repeat themselves in shopping centers across America suddenly seem to eat their young clientele, and, in a kind of perverse symbiosis, the kids feed upon the very forces that draw out their lifeblood.

The acting in *Zombie Night Five* is superb. The final twist is fittingly ironic, and some of the characters undergo complex personality shifts. The zombies, their flesh in the process of _____ (PUTR), are disgusting enough to keep you up at night. All in all, the film is _____ (OL) of the director's early masterpieces and is destined to become a classic itself.

1. What is the purpose of the second paragraph?
   A. to explain the plot of the movie
   B. to describe a scene that supports the author's point
   C. to summarize the larger message about religious conflicts
   D. to recommend *Zombie Night Five*

2. The tone of this passage could best be described as
   A. persuasive.
   B. apologetic.
   C. descriptive.
   D. informative.

3. According to the passage, *Zombie Night Five* is
   A. like some of the director's early work.
   B. totally unlike anything the director has ever done.
   C. predicable, like the director's early work.
   D. unlike anything the critic has ever seen.

Exercise VI. Drawing on your knowledge of roots and words in context, read the following selection and define the italicized word. If you cannot figure out the meaning of the word on your own, look it up in a dictionary. Note that the suffix *escent* means "growing, increasing."

Opponents of the new factory have exaggerated its environmental effect. They paint a bleak picture of polluted water in which nothing remains but the *putrescent* remains of animals and plants. In actuality, the factory will have strict safeguards to prevent its harming the surrounding area.

VOCABULARY WORD LIST FOR BOOKS IN THIS SERIES

Level VII
abbreviate
abduct
absolute
accessible
accompaniment
adjacent
aerate
aerial
affection
affirmative
agenda
airy
alleviate
ambition
analogy
apologetic
appendix
application
apprehend
ascertain
asocial
aspire
associate
assumption
attentive
attractive
ballistic
biographical
brevity
brutality
brute
capacity
capitalize
captivate
celebrant
celebratory
celebrity
certainty
certify
circumstance
coagulate
companionship
complex
composition
comprehend
compute
concerted
condense
conduct
confidante
confident
confirm
conscience
conservative
constant
constrict
consume
contract
convection
convict
cooperate
course
creed
currency
decapitate
deficient
deflate
defunct

deliverance
delude
denounce
density
deposit
descriptive
diagram
discount
discredit
disintegrate
dismantle
dispense
distract
domestic
domicile
dominate
dominion
duplicate
effortless
elevate
elongate
emaciated
emancipate
encompass
evaluate
evict
exhilarating
expire
fabled
fabulous
facsimile
fortify
fortitude
frugal
fruitful
gradual
grave
gravity
hilarity
host
hostile
hyperventilate
ideal
idealistic
idealize
illogical
illusion
impermanent
impress
incredible
infirm
inflate
inoperable
integrate
integrity
intend
invalid
invaluable
jubilant
jubilee
leverage
levitate
liberal
liberate
linguistic
literal
literate
malfunction
mantled

manual
manufacture
manuscript
meager
militant
militarize
multilingual
mythical
mythology
narrate
narrative
obliterate
observant
occurrence
omnipotent
operational
opponent
oppress
oral
oration
oratory
parable
passable
petrify
possessive
potent
preservation
presumptuous
procession
produce
program
progression
projectile
prolong
pronounce
proposition
prosecute
rapidity
rapture
recipient
recount
recurrent
regal
regicide
reign
remnant
reputation
restriction
reveal
savor
savvy
scientific
sensation
sensible
sentimental
sequel
sequence
sociable
socialize
solution
spirited
stationary
status
subject
subscribe
succession
suffice
sumptuous
suspend

symbolize
textile
texture
transact
transgress
transit
unveil
validate
vehicle
ventilate
victorious

Level VIII
abhor
abundant
accelerated
administer
admission
advisable
agile
agitate
allege
amnesty
anarchy
annals
annual
annuity
antediluvian
anticipate
appreciative
arbiter
arbitrary
arbitrate
archaic
arid
aspersion
assiduous
astronomical
autonomous
avail
castigate
cataclysmic
celestial
censor
censure
chastened
chastise
chronic
chronology
cloister
cohabitation
commensurate
composure
conceive
condone
confines
connoisseur
consolidate
conspicuous
contemporaneous
contemporary
corroborate
deceptive
deify
deign
deity
deluge
demented
demote

depreciate
derivative
desist
despicable
deter
detract
diagnosis
differentiate
dilute
dimension
disclose
discourse
disdain
disperse
dissident
donor
durable
duration
editorial
emergent
enact
enduring
energetic
enumerate
ergonomic
evident
exaggerated
exceptional
excursion
exhibit
exhume
exponential
extol
extract
finite
formidable
forte
fortitude
founder
frequent
fugitive
fundamental
fusion
horrific
humility
hypothesis
idiom
idiosyncrasy
immense
immerse
immovable
imposition
impunity
inconstant
indeterminate
indignant
infrequent
ingest
innumerable
inoculate
insidious
instantaneous
insular
insulate
inter
intercept
interminable
intersperse
intimidate

intrepid
intuitive
inveterate
invigorate
irreverent
jurisdiction
jurisprudence
litigant
litigation
magisterial
magistrate
matriarch
mentality
minister
mnemonic
mobile
monotheism
nebulous
nemesis
nimbus
nonplussed
nontraditional
notorious
ocular
omission
pantheon
parenthetical
participant
perjure
persistent
plurality
polytheistic
preliminary
preside
prodigal
prognosis
punitive
ration
rational
reactionary
reconnaissance
redundant
reference
refine
refuge
refuse
reinstate
repository
residual
respective
revere
revise
rivulet
robust
sanctify
sanctions
sanctuary
sanctum
seclude
sedentary
single
singular
solidarity
sparse
stellar
subliminal
submerge
submissive
subpoena

subsidiary
subsist
subterfuge
subterranean
suggestible
supersede
surgical
surplus
suspect
syndicate
synthesize
tempo
terminal
terrestrial
terrorize
timorous
torrent
torrid
trepidation
tutelage
unrivaled
valiant
valor
veteran
vigorous
vista
volatile

Level IX
abjure
abstain
accord
adept
affable
affiliate
affluent
agenda
alias
alienate
allegation
alleviate
alteration
altercation
alternate
amble
ambulatory
amiable
amicable
analogous
animosity
anonymous
antagonist
antagonize
antebellum
antibiotic
antonym
aptitude
aristocracy
assonance
audit
auditory
bellicose
belligerence
benefactor
benevolent
benign
bibliophile
biodegradable
bureaucrat

138

cadence	inconsequential	precept	adherent	derogatory	incoherent	protracted
casualty	incorporate	precise	admonition	despondent	incredulous	provincial
cede	incur	preclude	adverse	destitute	incriminate	punctilious
circumspect	indecisive	predominant	advocate	deviate	incursion	pungent
cognitive	indict	prefigure	aesthetic	diaphanous	indoctrinate	purported
cognizant	indomitable	privileged	anatomy	dichotomy	indolent	putrefy
collapse	ineffable	proactive	anesthetic	dictate	indubitable	putrid
concession	inept	progenitor	annotate	diffident	induce	rancid
confound	infantile	progeny	antipathy	diffuse	inference	rancor
conjure	infuse	prohibit	apathetic	diligent	infinite	rationale
consecutive	inhibit	prologue	apolitical	dismissive	infinitesimal	rationalize
cordial	iniquity	pronouncement	apparition	dispute	inflection	recollect
corporeal	injunction	propel	approbation	disreputable	inflexible	reconcile
corpulent	invidious	prospect	arrogant	dissolute	infraction	recourse
courier	invoke	protagonist	aspect	dissuade	infrastructure	recrimination
decadent	leaven	providential	avarice	docile	infringe	redolent
delegate	legacy	provocative	avid	doctrine	ingrate	redoubtable
denomination	legislative	rapacious	benediction	doleful	ingratiate	remiss
deplete	legitimize	rapt	bibulous	dolorous	inherent	reprobate
dialogue	levity	recant	cautionary	dubious	innovative	reprove
dictum	lucid	recede	cautious	effervescent	inquisitive	requisition
digress	magnanimous	recurrent	circumvent	effusive	insipid	resolute
dilate	magnate	reform	civic	egress	insoluble	restitution
diminish	magnitude	regress	civility	eloquent	intact	retort
discord	malevolent	rejoinder	civilize	emissary	intemperate	retract
disenchanted	malicious	relapse	clamorous	emote	interrogate	retrospective
dismal	maternal	relative	colloquial	empathy	intractable	revert
dispel	matriculate	renounce	compel	envisage	introspective	sacrilege
disposition	matron	replete	complacent	epiphany	invincible	sapient
dissemble	maxim	repulsion	comportment	epitome	irrational	sentient
dissonance	megalomaniac	resonant	compunction	equivocate	locution	sentiment
divest	megalopolis	retinue	conciliatory	errant	malediction	sentinel
domineering	mellifluous	revival	concise	erroneous	malodorous	stagnant
edict	metabolism	revoke	conducive	espouse	mea culpa	stagnate
effigy	metamorphosis	semblance	confer	evince	motif	stature
elapse	metaphorical	simulate	confide	evocative	motive	subvert
elucidate	microcosm	sophisticate	congress	evolve	novel	sycophant
enamored	microscopic	sophistry	conjecture	exacerbate	novice	tactile
enjoin	miniscule	sophomoric	connotation	excise	obviate	tangible
enunciate	minute	specter	conscientious	exclamatory	odoriferous	temper
equanimity	misinformation	suffuse	constructive	excruciating	olfactory	temperance
equilibrium	monogamy	superfluous	construe	exonerate	onerous	tome
equitable	monolithic	superlative	convene	expel	onus	tortuous
exacting	monologue	surreptitious	convoluted	expound	palatable	ultimate
execution	monopolize	susceptible	correspond	extort	palate	ultimatum
expatriate	morbid	sustain	cosmopolitan	facile	pandemic	unconscionable
expedient	moribund	symbiotic	counsel	facsimile	pathos	viaduct
figment	mortify	synonymous	covenant	factotum	penultimate	virile
filial	nomenclature	tenacious	credence	fallacious	perspicacious	virtue
formative	nominal	theocracy	credible	fallacy	persuasion	virtuoso
genealogy	noxious	translucent	credulity	fallible	petulant	visage
gradualism	omnivorous	travesty	crucial	fervent	phenomenon	voluble
herbivorous	partisan	unanimous	crux	fervor	placebo	
homogenized	paternal	uniform	culpable	fetid	placid	**Level XI**
homonym	patricide	unison	culprit	fidelity	politicize	ablution
immortalize	patronize	vested	cursory	fractious	precarious	abominable
impart	pedagogue	vestment	declaim	glut	precaution	abomination
impartial	pedant	vivacious	decriminalize	glutton	precursor	accede
impediment	pedestrian	vivid	deduce	gratuitous	premonition	acclivity
implement	perceptible	voracious	defer	gustatory	prescient	acquiesce
impose	perjury		deference	gusto	presentiment	adorn
improvise	pernicious	**Level X**	definitive	imbibe	primacy	adventitious
inalienable	philanthropy	aberrant	deflect	impervious	primal	alluvial
inaudible	philosophical	abject	degrade	impetuous	primeval	ambiance
incantation	phosphorescent	abrogate	dejected	impetus	proffer	annex
incision	photogenic	acerbic	demagogue	imprecation	proficient	antecedent
inclusive	phototropic	acquisitive	demographic	impulse	profuse	appall
incognito	posit	acrid	denotation	impute	proliferate	append
inconclusive	preamble	acrimonious	deprecate	incisive	proponent	appraise

appreciable
apropos
ascertain
assertion
attrition
auspices
auspicious
bacchanal
bacchic
belabor
candid
candor
catholic
cavernous
certitude
circuitous
communal
concave
conferment
conflagration
congested
consort
consortium
consummate
contort
contravene
contrite
converge
crevasse
crevice
declivity
decorous
decorum
demerit
demonstrative
denigrate
depose
deracinate
desolate
destine
desultory
detrimental
detritus
discomfit
disconcert
disseminate
dissertation
distill
distort
diverge
divulge
ecstasy
edification
elaborate
elegiac
elegy
entity
eradicate
essence
euphoria
excavate
excommunicate
exertion
expendable
extant
exultant
feasible
festoon

fete
fission
fissure
flagrant
flamboyant
florid
flourish
fluctuate
fluent
formality
formulaic
formulate
fortuitous
fortuity
fulminate
germane
germinal
germinate
gestate
gesticulate
hiatus
hoi polloi
holistic
illustrative
illustrious
impair
impeccable
impending
implicit
importunate
importune
incandescent
incendiary
incense
incommunicado
inexplicable
inflammatory
inordinate
insinuate
instill
insufferable
interject
inundate
irradicable
jocose
jocular
laborious
lachrymal
lachrymose
languid
languish
languor
lavish
lenient
lenitive
lethargy
liaison
ligature
liturgy
livid
luster
magnum opus
malaise
malfeasance
malign
malinger
meander
meretricious

meritorious
metaphrase
modus operandi
mollify
monosyllabic
monotone
monotonous
munificent
negate
negligent
negligible
nexus
obligatory
ominous
opulent
ordain
orifice
ornate
orotund
pallid
pallor
paradigm
paraphrase
parcel
parse
parvenu
peccadillo
peccant
pejorative
periphery
phraseology
plaint
plaintive
polyglot
polymath
precedent
predestination
preferential
preordained
proclivity
propitiate
propitious
quintessential
quittance
rapport
redound
refulgent
remonstrate
remunerate
repartee
requiem
resilient
restive
riparian
rudiment
rudimentary
sedition
semantic
seminal
semiotic
sinuous
soliloquy
solipsism
somnolent
sopor
soporific
stanch
stasis

static
staunch
subjective
suborn
summation
surfeit
synergy
totalitarian
totality
transitory
trenchant
trite
truncate
undulate
verdant
verdure
vigilant
vigilante
viridity
vulgar

Level XII
abscond
abstruse
adduce
adjourn
adjudicate
adroit
adumbrate
aggregate
agrarian
alacrity
allocate
allude
amoral
anachronism
anathema
animadversion
aperture
apocryphal
apposite
apprise
artifice
artless
ascribe
aspire
assay
asset
attenuate
avocation
bucolic
capitulate
caprice
celerity
chronicle
circumlocution
circumscribe
cogent
cognate
colloquy
collusion
complicity
composite
comprise
concede
concordance
concur
confluence

conjugal
consecrate
consign
conspire
constrain
contend
context
contiguous
contingent
covert
cryptic
defray
degenerate
demise
demur
demure
derisive
devoid
diabolical
discern
discordant
discrete
discretion
discursive
distend
diurnal
dour
duplicitous
duress
dystopian
egregious
emblematic
emulate
engender
ensue
episodic
epithet
esprit
evanescent
execrable
exigent
expiate
explicate
extemporaneous
extenuating
feign
felicitous
felicity
fictive
flux
fruition
fruitless
genre
gregarious
hyperbole
icon
iconoclast
iconography
idyllic
impious
implicate
in lieu of
inanimate
incessant
incite
inconsolable
incorrigible
incurious

inert
inexplicable
infelicitous
influx
infrangible
inimitable
innate
innocuous
insatiable
insuperable
intercede
interlude
internecine
interpose
intransigent
intrusive
inveigh
irrepressible
judicious
locus
loquacious
ludicrous
magniloquent
methodical
moratorium
mores
morose
myopic
nascent
obdurate
obloquy
obsequious
obtrusive
ostensible
overt
parturient
pastoral
peregrination
perpetuate
perpetuity
pertinacious
perturb
plenary
plenipotentiary
portend
precipitate
prestige
pretext
procure
proscribe
proviso
psyche
psychosomatic
psychotic
purveyor
purview
pusillanimous
recapitulate
recondite
rectify
rectitude
refract
remit
repast
repertory
reprehensible
reprimand
reserved

resignation
resuscitate
reticent
risible
rustic
sacrosanct
salubrious
salutary
salutation
satiety
sectarian
segue
servile
signatory
sinecure
sojourn
solace
solicitous
sovereign
stricture
stringent
subdue
subjugate
subservient
subtext
succor
suffrage
suppress
surfeit
surmise
synchronous
synod
synopsis
tacit
taciturn
temporal
temporize
tenable
tendentious
tenet
tenuous
topical
traduce
transect
transfigure
transpire
turbid
turbulent
umbrage
univocal
utopian
vacuity
vacuous
vaunted
vehement
verbatim
verbiage
verbose
vocation
vociferous